George Santayana

Consulting Editors

Hispanics of Achievement

George Santayana

David Carter

Chelsea House Publishers
New York   Philadelphia

CHELSEA HOUSE PUBLISHERS

Editor-in-Chief: Remmel Nunn
Managing Editor: Karyn Gullen Browne
Copy Chief: Mark Rifkin
Picture Editor: Adrian G. Allen
Art Director: Maria Epes
Assistant Art Director: Noreen Romano
Manufacturing Director: Gerald Levine
Systems Manager: Lindsey Ottman
Production Manager: Joseph Romano
Production Coordinator: Marie Claire Cebrián

Hispanics of Achievement
Senior Editor: John W. Selfridge

Staff for GEORGE SANTAYANA
Copy Editor: Benson D. Simmonds
Editorial Assistant: Danielle Janusz
Picture Researcher: Lisa Kirchner
Designer: Robert Yaffe
Cover Illustration: Bryn Barnard

3 5 7 9 8 6 4 2

Library of Congress Cataloging-in-Publication Data
Carter, David A.
    George Santayana/David Carter.
        p. cm.—(Hispanics of achievement)
    Includes bibliographical references and index.
    Summary: A biography of the Spanish-born philosopher and
author.
    ISBN 0-7910-1254-9
        0-7910-1281-6 (pbk.)
    1. Santayana, George, 1863–1952—Juvenile literature 2. Philoso-
phers—United States—Biography—Juvenile literature. [Santayana,
George, 1863–1952. 2. Philosophers.] I. Title. II. Series
B945.S24C37 1992   91-18015
191—dc20   CIP
    [B]   AC

Table of Contents

Hispanics of Achievement

Oscar Arias Sánchez
Costa Rican president

Joan Baez
Mexican-American folksinger

Rubén Blades
Panamanian lawyer and entertainer

Jorge Luis Borges
Argentine writer

Juan Carlos
King of Spain

Pablo Casals
Spanish cellist and conductor

Miguel de Cervantes
Spanish writer

Cesar Chavez
Mexican-American labor leader

El Cid
Spanish military leader

Roberto Clemente
Puerto Rican baseball player

Plácido Domingo
Spanish singer

El Greco
Spanish artist

Gloria Estefan
Cuban-American singer

Gabriel García Márquez
Colombian writer

Raul Julia
Puerto Rican actor

José Martí
Cuban revolutionary and poet

Rita Moreno
Puerto Rican singer and actress

Pablo Neruda
Chilean poet and diplomat

Antonia Novello
U.S. surgeon general

Octavio Paz
Mexican poet and critic

Javier Pérez de Cuéllar
Peruvian diplomat

Anthony Quinn
Mexican-American actor

Diego Rivera
Mexican artist

Linda Ronstadt
Mexican-American singer

Antonio López de Santa Anna
Mexican general and politician

George Santayana
Spanish poet and philosopher

Junípero Serra
Spanish missionary and explorer

Lee Trevino
Mexican-American golfer

Pancho Villa
Mexican revolutionary

CHELSEA HOUSE PUBLISHERS

INTRODUCTION

Hispanics of Achievement

Rodolfo Cardona

The Spanish language and many other elements of Spanish culture are present in the United States today and have been since the
country's earliest beginnings. Some of these elements have come
directly from the Iberian Peninsula; others have come indirectly, by
way of Mexico, the Caribbean basin, and the countries of Central
and South America.

Spanish culture has influenced America in many subtle ways,
and consequently many Americans remain relatively unaware of
the extent of its impact. The vast majority of them recognize the
influence of Spanish culture in America, but they often do not
realize the great importance and long history of that influence.
This is partly because Americans have tended to judge the Hispanic
influence in the United States in statistical terms rather than
to look closely at the ways in which individual Hispanics have
profoundly affected American culture. For this reason, it is fitting

that Americans obtain more than a passing acquaintance with the origins of these Spanish cultural elements and gain an understanding of how they have been woven into the fabric of American society.

It is well documented that Spanish seafarers were the first to explore and colonize many of the early territories of what is today called the United States of America. For this reason, students of geography discover Hispanic names all over the map of the United States. For instance, the Strait of Juan de Fuca was named after the Spanish explorer who first navigated the waters of the Pacific Northwest; the names of states such as Arizona (arid zone), Montana (mountain), Florida (thus named because it was reached on Easter Sunday, which in Spanish is called the feast of Pascua Florida), and California (named after a fictitious land in one of the first and probably the most popular among the Spanish novels of chivalry, *Amadis of Gaul*) are all derived from Spanish; and there are numerous mountains, rivers, canyons, towns, and cities with Spanish names throughout the United States.

Not only explorers but many other illustrious figures in Spanish history have helped define American culture. For example, the 13th-century king of Spain, Alfonso X, also known as the Learned, may be unknown to the majority of Americans, but his work on the codification of Spanish law has greatly influenced the evolution of American law, particularly in the jurisdictions of the Southwest. For this contribution a statue of him stands in the rotunda of the Capitol in Washington, D.C. Likewise, the name Diego Rivera may be unfamiliar to most Americans, but this Mexican painter influenced many American artists whose paintings, commissioned during the Great Depression and the New Deal era of the 1930s, adorn the walls of government buildings throughout the United States. In recent years the contributions of Puerto Ricans, Mexicans, Mexican Americans (Chicanos), and Cubans in American cities such as Boston, Chicago, Los Angeles, Miami, Minneapolis, New York, and San Antonio have been enormous.

The importance of the Spanish language in this vast cultural complex cannot be overstated. Spanish, after all, is second only to English as the most widely spoken of Western languages within the United States as well as in the entire world. The popularity of the Spanish language in America has a long history.

In addition to Spanish exploration of the New World, the great Spanish literary tradition served as a vehicle for bringing the language and culture to America. Interest in Spanish literature in America began when English immigrants brought with them translations of Spanish masterpieces of the Golden Age. As early as 1683, private libraries in Philadelphia and Boston contained copies of the first picaresque novel, *Lazarillo de Tormes*, translations of Francisco de Quevedo's *Los Sueños*, and copies of the immortal epic of reality and illusion *Don Quixote*, by the great Spanish writer Miguel de Cervantes. It would not be surprising if Cotton Mather, the arch-Puritan, read *Don Quixote* in its original Spanish, if only to enrich his vocabulary in preparation for his writing *La fe del cristiano en 24 artículos de la Institución de Cristo, enviada a los españoles para que abran sus ojos* (The Christian's Faith in 24 Articles of the Institution of Christ, Sent to the Spaniards to Open Their Eyes), published in Boston in 1699.

Over the years, Spanish authors and their works have had a vast influence on American literature—from Washington Irving, John Steinbeck, and Ernest Hemingway in the novel to Henry Wadsworth Longfellow and Archibald MacLeish in poetry. Such important American writers as James Fenimore Cooper, Edgar Allan Poe, Walt Whitman, Mark Twain, and Herman Melville all owe a sizable debt to the Spanish literary tradition. Some writers, such as Willa Cather and Maxwell Anderson, who explored Spanish themes they came into contact with in the American Southwest and Mexico, were influenced less directly but no less profoundly.

Important contributions to a knowledge of Spanish culture in the United States were also made by many lesser known individuals—teachers, publishers, historians, entrepreneurs, and others—with a love for Spanish culture. One of the most significant of these contributions was made by Abiel Smith, a Harvard College graduate of the class of 1764, when he bequeathed stock worth $20,000 to Harvard for the support of a professor of French and Spanish. By 1819 this endowment had produced enough income to appoint a professor, and the philologist and humanist George Ticknor became the first holder of the Abiel Smith Chair, which was the very first endowed Chair at Harvard University. Other illustrious holders of the Smith Chair would include the poets Henry Wadsworth Longfellow and James Russell Lowell.

A highly respected teacher and scholar, Ticknor was also a collector of Spanish books, and as such he made a very special contribution to America's knowledge of Spanish culture. He was instrumental in amassing for Harvard libraries one of the first and most impressive collections of Spanish books in the United States. He also had a valuable personal collection of Spanish books and manuscripts, which he bequeathed to the Boston Public Library.

With the creation of the Abiel Smith Chair, Spanish language and literature courses became part of the curriculum at Harvard, which also went on to become the first American university to offer graduate studies in Romance languages. Other colleges and universities throughout the United States gradually followed Harvard's example, and today Spanish language and culture may be studied at most American institutions of higher learning.

No discussion of the Spanish influence in the United States, however brief, would be complete without a mention of the Spanish influence on art. Important American artists such as John Singer Sargent, James A. M. Whistler, Thomas Eakins, and Mary Cassatt all explored Spanish subjects and experimented with Spanish techniques. Virtually every serious American artist living today has studied the work of the Spanish masters as well as the great 20th-century Spanish painters Salvador Dalí, Joan Miró, and Pablo Picasso.

The most pervasive Spanish influence in America, however, has probably been in music. Compositions such as Leonard Bernstein's *West Side Story*, the Latinization of William Shakespeare's *Romeo and Juliet* set in New York's Puerto Rican quarter, and Aaron Copland's *Salon Mexico* are two obvious examples. In general, one can hear the influence of Latin rhythms—from tango to mambo, from guaracha to salsa—in virtually every form of American music.

This series of biographies, which Chelsea House has published under the general title HISPANICS OF ACHIEVEMENT, constitutes further recognition of—and a renewed effort to bring forth to the consciousness of America's young people—the contributions that Hispanic people have made not only in the United States but throughout the civilized world. The men and women who are featured in this series have attained a high level of accomplishment in their respective fields of endeavor and have made a permanent mark on American society.

The title of this series must be understood in its broadest possible sense: The term *Hispanics* is intended to include Spaniards, Spanish Americans, and individuals from many countries whose language and culture have either direct or indirect Spanish origins. The names of many of the people included in this series will be immediately familiar; others will be less recognizable. All, however, have attained recognition within their own countries, and often their fame has transcended their borders.

The series HISPANICS OF ACHIEVEMENT thus addresses the attainments and struggles of Hispanic people in the United States and seeks to tell the stories of individuals whose personal and professional lives in some way reflect the larger Hispanic experience. These stories are exemplary of what human beings can accomplish, often against daunting odds and by extraordinary personal sacrifice, where there is conviction and determination. Fray Junípero Serra, the 18th-century Spanish Franciscan missionary, is one such individual. Although in very poor health, he devoted the last 15 years of his life to the foundation of missions throughout California—then a mostly unsettled expanse of land— in an effort to bring a better life to Native Americans through the cultivation of crafts and animal husbandry. An example from recent times, the Mexican-American labor leader Cesar Chavez has battled bitter opposition and made untold personal sacrifices in his effort to help poor agricultural workers who have been exploited for decades on farms throughout the Southwest.

The talent with which each one of these men and women may have been endowed required dedication and hard work to develop and become fully realized. Many of them have enjoyed rewards for their efforts during their own lifetime, whereas others have died poor and unrecognized. For some it took a long time to achieve their goals, for others success came at an early age, and for still others the struggle continues. All of them, however, stand out as people whose lives have made a difference, whose achievements we need to recognize today and should continue to honor in the future.

George Santayana

George Santayana, professor of philosophy at Harvard University, in Cambridge, Massachusetts, resigned his post abruptly on June 6, 1912, at the age of 48. A sizable inheritance had suddenly freed him from the necessity of making a living and enabled him to contemplate a life of study, writing, and world travel.

CHAPTER ONE

A Decisive Letter

It was springtime in Paris when George Santayana, the distinguished professor of philosophy at Harvard University, sat down to
write the most important letter of his life, one he had long dreamed
of writing. He dated it June 6, 1912, and addressed it to Abbott
Lawrence Lowell, president of Harvard University.

Exactly four months before, a telegram had arrived in Windsor,
England, where Santayana was staying at the time, informing him
that his mother had died. She had been ill for years and was in her
eighties, so the news of her death was not a surprise. However, he
had learned subsequently that his mother left him a legacy of
$10,000. This was not a princely sum even in 1912, but it was
enough for Santayana to contemplate the life of freedom and travel
for which he had longed. Writing his letter of resignation was the
first step toward living this life.

Born in Madrid, Spain, during the American Civil War, George
Santayana came to America when he was eight years old. His father,
Agustín Santayana, and his mother, Josefina Borras Sturgis, wanted

to secure the best possible education for their son. Though George arrived in Boston speaking no English, he learned to speak it and read it from his half sister Susana. Within two years he was enrolled at the Boston Latin School, one of the oldest and most prestigious schools in America.

From Boston Latin he went directly to Harvard University. There he studied philosophy and earned his bachelor of arts, graduating summa cum laude (with highest honors). After receiving his doctorate from Harvard and having learned German, French, Latin, Italian, and classical Greek to complement his English and Spanish, he was offered a position at the university as instructor of philosophy. He accepted the offer quite indifferently, for he had already decided to study architecture at the Massachusetts Institute of Technology if Harvard did not offer him a position.

At first, his promotion within Harvard's philosophy department had been somewhat slow in coming. Santayana was not well liked by the president of Harvard, Charles Eliot, who thought Santayana spent too much time thinking and not enough time handling everyday administrative responsibilities. However, Santayana won the respect and support of his colleagues on the faculty and was appointed full professor in spite of Eliot's misgivings.

Dwight Street, Boston, Massachusetts. When the eight-year-old George Santayana arrived in Boston with his father in 1872, he was unhappy, feeling very much the outsider. This feeling of being a European abroad stayed with him throughout his life, and he never became an American citizen.

Charles Eliot, president of Harvard University from 1869 to 1909, was not a great admirer of Santayana's. A practical education reformer, Eliot believed that the purpose of learning was to prepare for a career, whereas Santayana was an advocate of learning for its own sake and the pleasures it afforded.

The position Santayana now filled had been held by William James—an internationally acclaimed philosopher and writer and one of the pioneers of the new science of psychology—who had recently retired from teaching. Because James was such a giant in the field, a great amount of prestige went along with Santayana's new position. In fact, at the time of Santayana's appointment, Harvard's department of philosophy was staffed by the distinguished philosophical thinkers of the time. For example, in addition to William James, the Harvard philosophy faculty included Josiah Royce and George H. Palmer. Santayana was in very prestigious company.

Santayana had also made quite a name for himself as a writer and scholar. He was the author of two books of poetry, a play, and several works of philosophy as well as literary criticism. One of his critical works, *Three Philosophical Poets: Lucretius, Dante, and Goethe*, had been chosen to appear as the first volume of the *Harvard Studies in Comparative Literature*. His most recent philosophical work, a five-volume set entitled *The Life of Reason*, had been very favorably received; one renowned American educator even proclaimed it the most significant work of its type in America. Santayana was no longer merely enjoying the glory of being associated with America's greatest philosophical lights; he had become one of them. Recognized as such, he had been elected to the American Academy and Institute of Arts and Letters, one of the greatest honors an American writer can receive, and had been awarded an honorary degree of doctor of letters from the University of Wisconsin.

It is fair to say that Santayana's career was at its height that day in Paris when he sat down to compose this very important letter, but the future looked bright as well. President Eliot had retired, and the new president, Lowell, greatly appreciated Santayana's work. Moreover, Lowell was making changes in university policy that delighted Santayana. It would seem that things could hardly be better for George Santayana. Still, he sat down and wrote a letter resigning his position.

Santayana's letter had a startling effect on the academic community. In fact, his resignation at the height of his career surprised and made such an impression on so many people that in later years a fable grew up around his leaving. It was said that one day, in the midst of lecturing to students, Santayana looked out the window in

Unlike President Eliot, the eminent American psychologist and philosopher William James, Santayana's teacher, appreciated Santayana's academic work. After 35 years of teaching, James, the leading figure in the pragmatist school of philosophy, retired, and Santayana filled the position left vacant by his former teacher.

an absent manner and then suddenly, silently, walked out of the classroom never to return. Of course, this is not at all how Santayana left Harvard, but the tale reflects the shock that was felt in many academic circles following his sudden departure.

Santayana's decision to resign a full professorship at one of America's oldest and most acclaimed institutions of learning at the height of his brilliant career shocked and puzzled many. But considering that Santayana was never quite at home in the United States, this decision is perhaps understandable. Uprooted from his homeland at the age of eight, taken on a trying sea voyage across the Atlantic, and forced to settle in a country where he knew no one and did not speak the native language, Santayana yearned to return to Europe from the moment he arrived in the New World. Transported from sunny, warm Catholic Spain, the young Santayana suddenly found himself in a cold northern land where Protestants were the majority. His sensibilities were decidedly Spanish. Indeed, throughout his long life he lived in many countries but would always retain his Spanish citizenship.

By resigning, Santayana had been true to his own heart. With the inheritance just left him by his mother, he would, as long as he economized, be able to live the life he had always wanted, one of traveling, reading, writing, and contemplating. He could not have known then that his greatest acclaim lay ahead—that he would be twice proclaimed the greatest living critic and be awarded the Gold Medal of the Royal Society of Literature in London, that he would write a best-selling novel, that his essays would be considered a lasting legacy of English literature, and that he would be numbered among the century's greatest writers of English prose. Moreover, his most important philosophical works would be written years after he resigned from Harvard.

Santayana had deep divisions within his being, but perhaps it was these very divisions that, in equipoise, made for a rich, fulfilling, and surprising life.

*Three-year-old George Santayana and his half sister Susana Sturgis,
in a portrait painted by his father, Agustín Santayana. As a child, the
future philosopher learned a great deal from Susana, who became his
English tutor.*

CHAPTER TWO

A Young Spaniard in Boston

In January 1864, in Madrid, Spain, Josefina Borras Sturgis and Agustín Ruiz de Santayana presented their newborn baby for christening. The child was George Santayana.

Santayana's parents had met years earlier in the Philippines. At that time, Josefina Sturgis was married to a Bostonian by the name of George Sturgis. (It was in memory of her first husband, in fact, that George Santayana was named.) Josefina Sturgis had five children with George Sturgis, but only three of them survived infancy. When George Sturgis became seriously ill, he asked his wife to see to it that their children were educated in America. She eventually moved to Madrid after his death. There she again met Agustín Santayana. They married and had a son, George, born December 16, 1863.

Around 1865, the family moved from Madrid to Ávila, an ancient walled city not far from Madrid, best known for its two famous saints, St. Teresa of Ávila and St. John of the Cross. George enjoyed the simplicity of life in Ávila but found the city to be sad. Ávila had dwindled from a once flourishing city of 30,000 to one of only 6,000 people and was mostly in ruins.

The greatest problem the Santayanas faced in Ávila was finding quality education for their children. Ávila was small, and in rural Spain in the 19th century educational opportunities were limited. So to ensure that their children received an adequate education, the family hired a private tutor from Germany. He was genial, but he ended up making romantic advances toward Susana, George's half sister, in the midst of her lessons and was dismissed.

Around this time there developed a degree of tension between George's parents. Though Agustín and Josefina Santayana had much in common, their differences often proved difficult to overcome. They were from very different cultural backgrounds. Though of pure Spanish blood, Josefina Sturgis had spent little time in Spain. Moreover, her family background was Catalan,

Josefina Santayana, George's mother, believed strongly in the value of learning and made sure that her children received the best possible education. Although Santayana loved his mother, he was closer to his father, whom he not only loved but admired.

Agustín Santayana, in a self-portrait. George Santayana inherited his love for the arts, languages, and literature from his father, who was an accomplished painter and translator of Roman classics. When Agustín Santayana left his family behind and returned to Spain in 1873, his son maintained a steady correspondence with him.

whereas her husband's family was from León and Castile, regions of Spain with different histories and traditions.

Mindful of her promise to her first husband, Josefina sent her oldest son, Roberto, to Boston for his education about two years after the family moved to Ávila. Members of the Sturgis family still lived in Boston and had given her money since her husband's death. Two years later, Josefina Santayana left for Boston herself, taking her daughters, Josefina and Susana, with her.

Agustín Santayana and his young son must have felt quite alone in Ávila at this time—that is, until George's uncle moved into the house with them along with his wife and daughter. The niece soon married and became pregnant, but she and the baby both died in childbirth. In the aftermath of this tragedy, the household broke up, and once again George and his father were left alone in the house.

George received a basic education between the ages of five and eight, mainly studying the *cartilla*, a kind of alphabet book, and also

In 1872, Agustín Santayana and his son, George, left Spain for Boston. A precocious child, the young Santayana spoke no English when he arrived in the United States but learned quickly, and within two years he was enrolled at the prestigious Boston Latin School.

the catechism. But it soon became clear that he would have to leave Ávila to receive a quality education. So, in 1872, Agustín Santayana and his eight-year-old son, George, departed for Boston.

After first traveling to Liverpool, England, father and son set sail on the steamship *Samaria* on July 4. Years later, Professor Santayana would still recall their arduous trip across the Atlantic. The vessel was old and decrepit, and George was seasick during most of the crossing.

Arriving in East Boston, George did not recognize Roberto, now called Robert by his family, 17 years old and pimple-faced. George's first impressions of America were not good ones. He looked at the pier where they landed, one supported by rickety-looking piles and covered with slime, and wondered why anyone would want to come to a place such as the United States.

What was life like for this family that had now moved piecemeal across the Atlantic? As he looked back from the perspective of old age, Santayana wrote in his autobiography, *Persons and Places*, that there existed a great division within the family because each member had different interests. One visitor who dined with the family remarked afterward that he felt as if he had eaten at a boardinghouse in which all the people at the same table were unrelated. Santayana blamed the tenor of life in America for this split in what in his words had once been "a true family." Leaving Spain had caused "a terrible moral disinheritance," he wrote, and he disparaged the "pettiness and practicality of outlook and ambition" he found in his new country.

Because George had arrived in America unable to speak English, he was placed in kindergarten. Although he was, at age nine, much older than the children in his class, it was suggested that this was the best way for him to learn. Of course, he learned little in kindergarten; it was really his half sister Susana who educated him during this time. He learned to speak excellent English very quickly. The Santayana household was bilingual, so George conversed in English with some members of the family and in Spanish with others. One member of the family whom George certainly spoke Spanish with was his father.

Like his son, Agustín Santayana was unhappy in America. Although he could read English, he was unable to speak it very well. He was also appalled by the weather in Boston and missed Ávila's pleasant, warm climate. Probably what upset him most, however, was his wife's obvious preference for the Sturgises. The combination of all these difficulties overwhelmed him, and one year after his arrival in Boston, Mr. Santayana sailed back to Spain to live out the rest of his days in Ávila.

This must have been extremely painful for his only son. George loved both of his parents, but he always felt closer to his father. George shared many of his father's values. Before going to the Philippines, Agustín Santayana had studied painting with a student of Francisco José de Goya's, the famous Spanish artist, as well as law. George's father had also translated all the tragedies of the Roman dramatist Seneca into verse. It is doubtless that Santayana's love of the arts and literature is in part a tribute to his father's passion for the same. Another trait Santayana inherited from his father was his frugal nature. Santayana recalls that when he once asked his father why he traveled third class, his response was simply that there was no fourth class. After Agustín Santayana returned to Ávila, he wrote to George often and strongly urged him to learn languages. His son would not disappoint him in this regard. Within a few years, George had become a good Latinist and studied French and classical Greek as well.

George grudgingly made his home in America. He was unhappy from the age of 8 until he was 16, keeping mostly to himself, living in his dreams and on a steady diet of books—not a surprising reaction for a child who was bright and sensitive and felt isolated.

In 1873, George was sent to a public grammar school, and the following year he began attending Boston Latin School. His mother knew that there he could receive an outstanding education, in fact the best then available in America. In addition to languages,

The Boston Latin School. Santayana was an excellent student at the competitive preparatory school. He studied mathematics and English and excelled especially in rhetoric, the art of public speaking.

he studied mathematics, English, and rhetoric. He excelled at rhetoric, the art of public speaking—a very popular subject in American schools during the 19th century.

Around this time, a young architect began courting Susana. He encouraged her to read *Stones of Venice,* a book by the English writer John Ruskin. She gave the book to George to read, and so began his lifelong passion for architecture. He read over and over the entry on architecture in their household encyclopedia. During these years before his adolescence, George spent many hours making detailed drawings of buildings, usually grand ones, such as palaces and cathedrals. He especially loved Gothic architecture.

Susana was important in George's life in many ways other than teaching him English and introducing him to architecture. In his autobiography he wrote that he had loved her more than anyone. He added that in many ways she played the role of his mother. She also instructed him in another aspect of life close to his heart as a youth—religion. Their points of view were dissimilar, however: Susana took a literal approach to religion, whereas for George religion was like poetry—beautiful and inspiring but not something to believe in any literal sense. He maintained that religion was like a great work of literature, humanizing and vitalizing and thus necessary for a full life.

On his own, George would occasionally attend an early mass at a Catholic church. Rising before the sun on a cold, blustery winter morning, he would walk through the empty streets of Boston. The world seemed ugly and boring to him, and he took refuge from its harshness in these walks to church, just as he had found solace in poetry and religion. That he did not believe in religion in any conventional sense created a deep spiritual conflict within Santayana that caused him great emotional pain. In anguish he pondered the dilemma: The world was real but ugly, whereas dreams were beautiful but not real. Torn between the world of objects and the world of dreams, Santayana wrote a poem, "At the Church Door," when he was about 15 years old. He described himself standing at the door of the church and looking inside, filled with regret at never being able to live on the inside of the church.

Throughout his youth, Santayana enjoyed Susana's company and continued to read books on religion and architecture. He also developed some close friendships during his last few years at the Boston Latin School and furthered his exploration of the world of literature. The kind of literature he preferred was poetry, and eventually his greatest ambition was to be a poet.

The earliest poems by Santayana that have survived were written when he was around 15 years old. His school began a publication, and he was named its first editor. His unsigned poems began to appear in its pages, and at 16 he won a school prize for a lengthy poem that described the superiority of nighttime over daytime. His talents were noticed when he won several additional prizes that same year, awarded on Honor's Day in June 1880, in the Boston Music Hall.

A mocking attitude was as essential a characteristic of George's makeup as intelligence or love of poetry. An episode in which he combined these three traits landed him in an embarrassing position with his teachers. His class had formed a club that met weekly to debate in an empty room opposite the Common in Boston. For one of their meetings, George had composed a satirical poem that poked fun at several of his teachers. The poem was such a hit with his schoolmates that they made copies of it. It had been intended only for other students' eyes, but it eventually became public. George dutifully went to see the headmaster at his home and apologized. It must have been an impressive apology, for the headmaster was not severe with him and told him only that he should write to the teachers mentioned in the poem to express his regrets. Luckily, this incident did not cause George to fall into disrepute with the school's administration. He was elected major by his fellow students for their school's battalion of the Boston School Regiment. Though they chose another student for the higher position of lieutenant colonel, the headmaster overruled the election and awarded George the higher rank.

The young Santayana capped off a year of accomplishment by receiving six honorable mentions in his Harvard entrance examinations. He spent the summer prior to entering Harvard reading *The Divine Comedy* by the Italian poet Dante, constantly comparing the English translation with the Italian version. It was clear to his teachers as well as his peers that George Santayana was destined to live a life of many accomplishments.

Santayana enrolled at Harvard University in 1882. At Harvard, Santayana sloughed off the alienation of his youth that had caused him to withdraw into books and long musings; he joined numerous clubs and socialized frequently.

CHAPTER THREE

An Ideal Student's Life

Santayana had few extra dollars to spend his first year at Harvard, so the room he rented that year was sparsely furnished and had no heat or water. In order to stay warm in winter, Santayana kept a coal fire burning throughout the night. Although he did have to fetch his own coal and water, he received the services of a "goody," or servant, who cleaned his room. He later wrote that his first year was miraculous in its economy.

Santayana soon found that the room of an undergraduate was not a very productive place in which to work because of the steady stream of interruptions and temptations, whether social, athletic, or academic. Consequently, he studied mainly in the university library. He found a favorite area near books on philosophy and periodicals from foreign countries. There he tended to browse freely. He wrote in his autobiography, "I don't think my time was wasted . . . my mind became accustomed to large horizons and to cultivated judgments."

A talented cartoonist, Santayana was a regular contributor to the Harvard Lampoon, *a popular college magazine. This cartoon, which pokes fun at the social norms of the upper class, is typical of Santayana's many contributions to the publication.*

Snodkins (with touching candor). IF I LOOK A LITTLE SHEEPISH, MISS ROSELEAF, AND MY FRIENDS TELL ME I DO, I ASSURE YOU IT ISN'T MY FAULT; IT IS BECAUSE MY CLOTHES ARE ALL WOOL.

One day, two seniors who were interested in learning more about Spain slid a note under Santayana's door and invited him to visit. Their ideas about Spain were rather romantic and were founded on popular fictional works they had read. The conversation, however, drifted to art, and, learning that Santayana liked to draw, one of the students suggested that he submit some artwork to the *Lampoon,* a famous satirical journal published by Harvard students. Santayana did so, and his work was accepted. He was elected to the board of the *Lampoon,* and over the next 3 years, more than 50 of his cartoons appeared in its pages. This connection with the publication held a greater impact for Santayana than just having his artwork published, for he became friends with two other freshmen who were elected to the board and through them met other students.

The cast of a production of the Hasty Pudding Play. While at Harvard, Santayana played roles in university theater productions, including the Hasty Pudding play, a comedy performed annually by Harvard students. Santayana is pictured in costume (a white dress), seated just right of center.

Soon he had many friends, and his past as a lonesome young boy became remote. During his student years at Harvard, Santayana became a member of a total of 11 clubs, including the Art Club, the Chess Club, and Phi Beta Kappa. He played leads in theater productions in 1884 and 1886; one role was in the Hasty Pudding Play, a humorous performance given annually at Harvard. Another club he joined, the O.K., gave dinners, and at these he read some of his poems. He was a founding member of the *Harvard Monthly* and president of the Philosophical Club.

Not only did Santayana form many friendships, but these social contacts helped refine his mind and tastes both as an undergraduate and afterward. His fellow student Charles Loeser became his friend because of a shared interest in literature and painting. Eventually, he instilled in Santayana a deeper understanding of Italy and its people, so that when Santayana settled there in later life, he was already very familiar with the country. With his friend Ward Thoron he read *War and Peace*, took walks, and read French books. This friendship contributed to Santayana's love for the French language and its literature.

In spite of all the social activity, his first year of college went well with one exception. He failed a course in algebra, but he took it again later and passed. He continued his study of Latin and Greek during his freshman year, work that would help lead him to his vocation.

At the end of his freshman year, Santayana received a pleasant surprise: His mother asked him to visit his father in Spain. Santayana's entire family knew that he longed to return to Europe to see its classical architecture and visit its old villages. Thus he began what was to be the first of many return trips to Europe. He sailed from New York on a steamship for Antwerp and was plagued with a terrible case of seasickness. A bed was placed on the ship's deck for him so he could at least have the benefit of fresh air and sun.

When he reached Ávila, he found his father relatively unchanged in appearance but somewhat deaf. The deafness was a problem for Santayana, who, having read hardly any Spanish books in the past 10 years, had lost his ability to express himself fluently in Spanish.

Santayana traveled within Spain while visiting his father. In Saragossa he stopped to admire the city's Gothic cathedral, with its

A member of as many as 11 clubs, Santayana (seated, center) was a founding member of the Harvard Monthly *and served as president of Harvard's Philosophical Club. Through his involvement in such social and academic organizations, Santayana made a name for himself and met many new friends.*

shrine of Spanish patriotism, *La Virgen del Pilar.* There he performed the customary act of kissing the revered pillar made of jasper. He also made a side trip to Tarragona, a seaport on the Mediterranean, to visit relatives. By the time he reached Tarragona, he was tired and feverish and found he could not eat the meal they had prepared as a welcome. He went directly to bed and was examined by a doctor, who announced that Santayana had smallpox. During his convalescence, he took walks with his father, and the two became even closer.

Once he fully recovered, Santayana resumed his travels. His father, hoping that Santayana might one day settle in Spain, paid for a trip to Madrid and instructed his son to call on an influential friend. However, the man was not in when Santayana visited, and nothing came of it. While in Madrid he visited the Prado, one of the world's greatest museums. Later, he toured Barcelona, Paris, and Lyons, where he went to the theater night after night to see the legendary actress Sarah Bernhardt.

George Santayana returned to classes for his sophomore year weak from smallpox and not improved by yet another case of seasickness on the return voyage. He immediately plunged into his studies, however, and signed up for a full load of demanding

Santayana greatly admired the work of Sarah Bernhardt, the French stage and screen actress, whom he saw perform in Lyons, France, during the 1880s. Like Santayana, Bernhardt was multitalented: Not only was she an acclaimed actress, but she was also a playwright, a poet, and a sculptress.

courses. From his sophomore year until he received his B.A., he studied mostly philosophy, English, and the classics, supplemented by classes in the natural sciences.

During his final years at Harvard, Santayana began to consider how he would earn a living after graduation. There does not seem to have been a particular moment when Santayana decided to become a philosopher; rather, the choice seems to be something he naturally gravitated toward. Perhaps it was to be expected for a young man who read classical Greek, the language of the Western world's greatest philosophers, and who had probed deeply into the world of dreams, religion, and poetry to seek answers in philosophy. The works of Baruch Spinoza, the 17th-century Dutch philosopher, also helped Santayana sort out various matters that preoccupied his thoughts. Santayana later credited Spinoza as a major influence on his work.

Knowledge of another classical language, Latin, also appears to have influenced Santayana's choice of career. One of the authors he had read on his own in Latin and immediately admired was the poet Lucretius. Santayana particularly liked the poet's notion of naturalism, the view that there is nothing except nature and therefore nothing supernatural exists. This belief later became one of the cornerstones of Santayana's own philosophy.

Of the great teachers in Harvard's philosophy department, it was William James who most influenced the young Santayana. With James, Santayana studied the works of the major figures in the history of philosophy, with a special emphasis on the empiricists David Hume and John Locke. The empiricists believed that all real knowledge is based on information received through the five human senses, that there are no innate ideas. The letters Santayana regularly received from his father were another important influence on his intellectual pursuits; news from his father was usually spiced with sharp opinions and observations about current events in Spain.

During his senior year of college, Santayana met and became good friends with one of his fellow students, Charles Augustus Strong. Strong and Santayana both studied philosophy, and together they founded the Philosophical Club at Harvard.

Although now a student of philosophy, Santayana still had not decided to become a professor of that subject. In fact, the idea was not at all attractive to him. What he felt in his heart was a desire to learn, especially through travel. "I loved speculation for itself, as I loved poetry, not out of worldly respect or anxiety lest I should be mistaken, but for the splendour of it, like the splendour of the sea and the stars," he wrote in *Persons and Places*. He added that he might easily have become a traveling student like those in the Middle Ages, going from one great center of learning to another and seeing the world along the way.

Again, money from a Sturgis family connection played a fateful role in the path his career would take. His mother received a sum of $500 a year from a relative of her first husband's and decided to give this money to her youngest son. Santayana, with a new allowance, began to plan what he would do next. There was a Walker Fellowship at Harvard for graduate study in Germany, and Santayana felt that his friend Charles Strong, the only other student who had applied for the fellowship besides Santayana, would

Santayana met and became close with Charles Strong, also a student of philosophy, during their senior year at Harvard. Together they founded Harvard's Philosophical Club.

probably win it. But Santayana knew that Strong, too, had an allowance. He proposed that they share the fellowship money, no matter which of them received it, so that they could both go to Germany. Strong readily agreed to the plan because he enjoyed discussing philosophy with his new friend. They approached their department about this, and the department agreed that they could share the fellowship. After receiving his B.A. summa cum laude in 1886, Santayana departed for Europe.

So eager was Santayana to travel that immediately upon finishing his last examination he departed for Germany. Once in Europe, he went to Ávila to visit his father. On the way, he passed through Spanish and French towns—Caen, Le Mans, Angers, Poitiers, Angoulême, and Bordeaux in France and Burgos in Spain—where he indulged his love of Gothic architecture by visiting their cathedrals.

That fall, Santayana took a room in a German boardinghouse in Göttingen, where he worked to improve his German. From Göttingen he went on to Dresden and continued studying German with his friend Herbert Lyman, following a schedule that combined study with entertainment. In the morning they took a German lesson together and then went for a walk. In the evening they went to an opera or a play. From Dresden, Santayana continued on to Berlin to take classes at the university there.

An unresolved conflict from Santayana's high school days now resurfaced. As Santayana had neared graduating from high school, he had been in the grips of the struggle that moved him to write "At the Church Door"—the tension between the real world and his longing for an ideal one. Santayana wrote that as an undergraduate at Harvard this conflict had remained unresolved. In his autobiography he does not say exactly when he worked out a satisfactory resolution to his dilemma, but he does say it happened by the time he was a student traveling in Germany. He adopted a point of view that would provide the foundation for the entire system of philosophy he would eventually construct.

There had been no great change in sentiment. . . . Yet in
belief, in the clarification of my philosophy, I had taken an
important step. I no longer wavered between alternate views
of the world, to be put on or taken off like alternate plays at
the theater. I now saw that there was only one possible play,
the actual history of nature and of mankind, although there
might well be ghosts among the characters and soliloquies
among the speeches. Religions, *all* religions, and idealistic
philosophies, *all* idealistic philosophies, were the soliloquies
and the ghosts.

He added that although these "soliloquies" and "ghosts" might
be eloquent in expression and have profound insights that could
offer an excellent critique of the "play," still they remained only
parts of the drama. Their worth as criticism, however, was totally
dependent on their faithfulness to the facts of the play as well as to
the feelings experienced by a critic viewing the play.

In Dresden, Santayana took a course in Greek ethics that
proved crucial to his resolution of this conflict. The classical era in
Greece produced numerous literary masterpieces of Western civil-
ization. After reading these works, Santayana came to conclude that
much of the reason for their greatness sprang from the Greeks'
naturalistic view of the world, a view that recognized the divine in
the logic and beauty of nature. Santayana never desired to be inside
a church again, believing that God was truly everywhere to be
experienced.

Before Santayana became acquainted with the Greek classics,
Santayana's father had planted the seeds of his son's attraction to
naturalistic religion. Santayana relates the following story as an
example of how his father's view of things influenced him: One day,
while walking with his father, Santayana saw a pile of large, unusual-
ly shaped boulders grouped in a formation that looked fantastic.
Santayana remarked to his father that it was too bad that there was
not a geologist on hand who could enlighten them about how such
a formation came to exist. His father retorted that it would be of no

use, for the geologist could expound his theory but would not have been there to witness what had happened. After recounting this story, Santayana wrote, "I have made the authority of things, as against the presumption of words or ideas, a principle of my philosophy."

Santayana believed that humankind was the source and measure of good and evil. In other words, morality has its origin and measure in human nature. Santayana also believed that the forces that govern mankind are the forces of nature. For Santayana, nature is great and man is small. In the face of these powers, he maintained, we should be humble, even pious. Santayana believed that even the human mind is an offspring of nature's powers. Although Santayana did not believe in any religion literally, his life was a sustained meditation on the truths of religion, and given his beliefs about nature, he was very sympathetic to pantheism, which identifies God with the natural world. Santayana's philosophy has been described as having an astonishing coherence. This may be because he had all of his most fundamental insights as a young man and spent the rest of his life formulating a philosophy based on those insights.

After his first semester at Dresden, Santayana, with Strong, decided to go to England. Santayana was interested in seeing the architecture of England as well as meeting its people. He was not disappointed, and this visit was the beginning of a lifelong fascination with that country. He and Strong rented rooms in Oxford and lived in a manner typical of all Santayana's student years, enjoying reading, eating, talking, walking, and socializing.

One of the more colorful Englishmen Santayana would ever meet was the poet and critic Lionel Johnson. When Santayana went to call on Johnson at his apartment, prominent on a table in the center of one of his rooms were a jug of whiskey and two open books of poetry. On the walls hung portraits of two cardinals; in fact, during the conversation, Johnson announced his intention to convert to Catholicism. Johnson informed Santayana that he ate only eggs in the morning and consumed nothing for the remainder of the day but tea. Exceptions to this rule were the rare occasions when he went on a long walk in the country, after which he ate dinner. Despite Johnson's eccentricities, Santayana considered him a genius, and the two became friends. In fact, Johnson later honored Santayana with two poems, "Satanas," which is expressly dedicated to Santayana, and "To a Spanish Friend."

Writing his own poetry continued to consume much of Santayana's energy. Most of his poems were comic in nature, but he also experimented with many verse forms, including his eventual favorite, the sonnet.

In 1887, Santayana made his third return visit to Spain. Susana had decided to move to Spain permanently, and Santayana went to Gibraltar to meet her. It still seemed possible then that Santayana might settle in Spain. Whatever his future intent with regard to Spain, Santayana feared that his German was inadequate to prepare for a Ph.D. in Berlin. He decided to return to Harvard to write his dissertation, and then, unless offered a chance to teach somewhere, he would go to the Massachusetts Institute of Technology to study architecture. Returning to the United States to study for a Ph.D. would violate all the rules of the Walker Fellowship. Still, Santayana insisted to William James that he must do so. He felt he could work to better purpose and in a more concentrated way in English in the United States. Finally, the department was willing to grant this concession, for they thought so highly of him.

Back at Harvard, Santayana worked on his dissertation. The subject of his study was Rudolf Hermann Lotze, a 19th-century philosopher who questioned the value of formal logic for the purposes of philosophical investigation. Although there are both similarities and differences between Santayana's and Lotze's points of view, certainly they both doubted the usefulness of formal logic. In 1889, Santayana completed his doctoral dissertation and received his Ph.D. His formal education complete, Santayana was as eager as ever to travel.

His doctoral dissertation complete, Santayana accepted an invitation to teach a course offered by the Harvard philosophy department in 1889. The course—a study of the British idealists and empiricists—had previously been taught by Santayana's mentor, William James.

CHAPTER FOUR

The Duties of Academia

Santayana might have become an architect if William James had not been overburdened with work and looking for someone to take over one of his teaching assignments. The course James wanted to hand over to another teacher was one on the work of John Locke, George Berkeley, and David Hume, philosophers Santayana had studied under James. Santayana was offered the position, and he accepted.

Santayana began teaching the class of only three or four students, and on the second day the small group met, the president of Harvard walked into the classroom unannounced. Santayana was startled but managed to rise out of respect for his visitor's high office. President Eliot told him that another professor had just resigned. Only three students were enrolled in one of his courses, but university policy was not to cancel any course that had been offered. Would Santayana be willing to teach that course as well? Santayana asked if he could think it over until the next morning.

Eliot agreed, and after reflection, Santayana decided to accept the second assignment.

Santayana and Eliot had very different views on the meaning of education, and these differences caused friction between them. For Santayana, education was an end in itself; the pursuit of learning was for its own sake and for the pleasures it afforded. Eliot, on the other hand, saw education mostly as a means to a professional career. One day, Eliot asked Santayana how his classes were progressing. Santayana answered that the students were making steady progress through Plato and would soon begin their study of Aristotle, naming two of the most important Greek philosophers. Eliot showed impatience with Santayana's response; what he had meant was, How many students had signed up for his courses? On another occasion, Eliot urged Santayana to "teach facts and not ideas."

If Santayana was at odds with the college administration, with his colleague William James he enjoyed a good working relationship. Given their similarities, it is not surprising that the two men highly valued each other. For example, both shared the view that philosophical argumentation was a literary endeavor, rejecting the use of strictly logical proofs, which were so often used by many academic philosophers. Also, they both believed that philosophy was really a way of life and not merely a subject to be taught at universities.

There are numerous accounts of how Santayana lived according to his philosophical ideals. As one story has it, when a painter was asked to do a group portrait of the Harvard philosophy department, the five distinguished scholars entered the room where the artist had prepared to work. However, when they were shown her preliminary sketch, it became clear that painting the portrait would not be an easy task. Josiah Royce resolutely refused to be in the center of the painting; William James did not wish to be portrayed in profile, as the artist had sketched him, arguing that having only one eye visible would make him seem less authoritative; George Palmer, who was short, insisted that he not be painted standing;

Hugo Munsterberg said that the plan of the painting must be changed so that he would be in the center front. Throughout these exchanges, Santayana sat apart and observed all the discussion. Finally, disgusted with the display of vanity and conceit, Santayana stood and said, "Whatever metaphysical egotism may assert, one cannot vote to be created," before walking out of the room.

In his autobiography, Santayana wrote that his first lectures went very poorly. If these lectures were in fact disappointing, there is no doubt that he eventually became an outstanding teacher, given the comments of his students. Among these students were many who became prominent in their respective fields. They included the poets Conrad Aiken, Wallace Stevens, and Robert Frost, the acclaimed journalist and editor Walter Lippmann, the Pulitzer Prize–winning historian Samuel Eliot Morison, and U.S. Supreme Court justice Felix Frankfurter. Walter Lippmann in fact changed his field of study to philosophy because of James and Santayana, and he considered the latter to be the better teacher. When he became editor of the *New Republic*, an important political magazine, Lippmann asked Santayana to write for it. The poet and literary critic T. S. Eliot was a lone dissenter among Santayana's former students, claiming that Santayana's lectures put him to sleep.

In 1890, Santayana moved into this room at 7 Stoughton Hall while launching his teaching career at Harvard. Among the ranks of Santayana's many students of distinction were the poets Conrad Aiken, Wallace Stevens, and Robert Frost.

One of the most widely read poets of his generation, Robert Frost used the images of his boyhood to weave deceptively simple verses. Although he wrote about idyllic life in rural New England, his deeper concern was the human predicament, with all its difficult trials, frustrations, and temptations. Frost won the Pulitzer Prize four times for his poetry.

As Santayana was learning how to teach, he kept up his usual full schedule of reading, writing poetry, and socializing. One of his most frequent activities apart from his professional duties was watching Harvard football and track practice sessions. In 1894, Santayana, a quiet sports enthusiast, wrote an essay entitled "Philosophy on the Bleachers." One critic called the piece "one of the

Another of Santayana's students was the American poet T. S. Eliot. Eliot wrote complicated verses in which he used images from the classics of Western literature, the philosophies of the Eastern mystics, and the characters of ancient mythologies to comment on what he perceived as the alienating quality of modern life.

best essays on sport." He also walked frequently to Brookline to visit his mother, who continued to speak Spanish, three times each week. He formed close friendships with a number of undergraduates. At the beginning of his teaching career, he was not much older than the students he taught. It is not surprising that some of the attachments he formed with these young men became very strong, for Santayana was homosexual.

For mostly three reasons, Santayana left little record of his romantic life. The first is that Santayana lived at a time when it was not considered proper for one to discuss one's sexuality openly with others. Even within one's own family, the topic of sex was usually not discussed between men and women. Second, there was great intolerance of homosexuals in America and Europe in Santayana's day. For example, Santayana was living in England when the Irish playwright Oscar Wilde, one of the 20th century's great literary talents, was tried by the English courts and sentenced to

Harvard Yard as seen from Santayana's room at Stoughton Hall. Although Santayana enjoyed teaching at first, he quickly grew tired of it and sought out other diversions. He continued to write poetry and to socialize often, and he also developed an interest in spectator sports, especially American football.

Like his Harvard classmate George Santayana, Warwick Potter was a lover of high culture and had a buoyant sense of humor. When Potter died in 1893, Santayana was traumatized, as the two men had for years been extremely close companions and confidants.

hard labor for having sex with men. The third reason is that Santayana had a marked distaste for literary confession.

Still, it is generally accepted that among the strongest emotions Santayana felt for any man were those he had for Warwick Potter, a student at Harvard. Potter was idealistic, a lover of culture, and much given to laughter. Santayana and his half sister Susana also loved to laugh, and Santayana felt that he could not have a true friendship with someone who did not have a good sense of humor. Potter and Santayana thus had a basis for a close and lasting relationship.

In 1893, personal loss struck Santayana. When he went to Ávila to visit his father, Santayana found to his dismay that his father was not only old but blind, deaf, and poor; not long after Santayana's arrival, his father died. That same year, Santayana received news that Warwick Potter had died of cholera in Germany. Santayana eloquently describes his reaction to Potter's death in his autobiography: "I was brimming over with the sense of parting, of being divided by fortune where at heart there was no division. I found myself, unwillingly and irreparably, separated from Spain, from England, from Europe, from my youth and from my religion." A third disappointment came next, but this one happened gradually, over a period of years. After moving to Spain, Susana married. Santayana objected to the marriage because at the age of 41 she was marrying a man who had 6 children by a previous marriage. He felt that she was marrying not for love but out of desperation and fear of spending her old age alone.

The combined effect of these events induced a crisis in Santayana's life. He wrote of the pain in his heart and of "a passage through dark night." As usual, he sought a philosophical solution. The lesson he learned from his terrible losses was that nothing in this world lasts forever, that one must inevitably lose that which one loves. He understood that if one lives in the world, personal loss and suffering are unavoidable.

When 41-year-old Susana Sturgis, Santayana's half sister, got married to a Spanish widower, Santayana was incensed. He saw the marriage not as an act of love but as one of desperation made out of a fear of being alone—an indication, he believed, that she lacked personal strength and a sense of independence.

The solution for Santayana was to live a bit less in the world, to turn away from life among people toward the inner life. He continued to teach, write poetry, travel, and correspond with friends, and on the surface his life changed little. But his outlook was different now, and this change would manifest itself over time. For example, he renounced material possessions and tried to live even more simply than he had in the past. For the rest of his life, Santayana lived an ascetic's life, never owning a house or apartment and accumulating little in the way of possessions other than a few pieces of furniture and a small collection of books. Out of his suffering came an inner peace, a falling away of desires, and the ability to be happy with very little.

In 1894, Santayana's first book, *Sonnets and Other Verses*, was published by a Massachusetts publisher. Reviews were mixed, but most were negative. One critic wrote that the author's attempt to write in a style of classical severity had resulted in poetry that was simply austere. It was around this time that Santayana concluded that an academic life was not conducive to writing and developing his philosophy. He began to set aside some money each year for his retirement.

The following year, he went on a trip to Italy with his friend Charles Loeser, who knew the country and spoke Italian well. Together they visited Venice, Florence, and Rome. Whenever the two of them traveled together, Santayana gave Loeser 20 gold francs each day. Loeser then took care of any daily expenses beyond this sum and made all the necessary arrangements.

During his tenure at Harvard, Santayana continued to write poetry, studied architecture and other arts, and became competent in several languages. He also developed an expertise in aesthetics, the study of the philosophy of art and beauty. He began teaching a course on aesthetics and then wrote down the contents of his lectures and offered the manuscript to various publishers. All rejected it. Finally, after he had given up hope that the book would be published, it was accepted by Charles Scribner's Sons. This began a relationship that would last nearly 60 years, the remainder of Santayana's life. The book, *The Sense of Beauty*, was praised by critics as a work of "perfection."

Santayana then took a year's leave from Harvard without salary. He returned to England. After a restful month, he left Oxford to read Plato and Aristotle at King's College in Cambridge. There he seemed to enjoy the traditional life of the academician, wearing a master's gown and dining at high table with the dons. He relished the opportunity to discuss philosophy with Oxford's eminent philosophers, among them Bertrand Russell, Santayana's cousin through his mother's first husband. Russell was not only a philosopher but a respected mathematician.

When he returned from England, Santayana found that the philosophy department had advanced his name for an assistant professorship. President Eliot was opposed. In a remarkable letter in which he compared the work of Santayana to that of a ditchdigger, Eliot made his point. Colleagues James and Royce weighed in behind Santayana, knowing that Santayana would resign if not

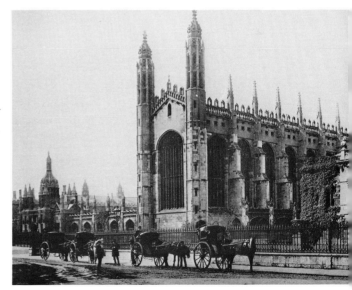

In 1896, Santayana went to England, where he read ancient Greek philosophy at King's College, Cambridge University. At Cambridge, he met one of the most influential thinkers of the 20th century, the Welsh mathematician and philosopher Bertrand Russell.

52

Bertrand Russell enrolled at Trinity College, Cambridge University, in 1890 and remained there as a fellow and a lecturer specializing in logic and epistemology until 1916, when he was dismissed for espousing socialist doctrine and opposing World War I. He returned to Trinity as a fellow in 1944.

given the promotion. Eliot gave in. In the next three years, Santayana published three books while continuing to teach and travel. He also made a good deal of progress on what would be a five-volume philosophical work of tremendous range.

The year after Santayana was promoted, Charles Scribner's Sons published his *Lucifer: A Theological Tragedy.* But the play was not very well received, and Santayana never attempted drama again. Santayana himself reviewed the play in the *Harvard Monthly,* apparently as a joke.

In 1898, the Spanish-American War took place. When the Spanish fleet at Santiago was destroyed, Admiral Sampson called the victory a Fourth of July present to the American people. Offended, Santayana wrote "Spain in America" in reply. The poem laments Spain's "sadness and dishonor" and was described by critics as a "moving and eloquent cry for a marriage of the two cultures, the spirits of the north and the south." Throughout his life, Santayana felt these two cultures pull him in opposite directions. He once expressed his frustration by saying that the result of his Latin heritage made him want "to say plausibly in English as many un-English things as possible."

In 1901, Santayana's second book of poetry appeared, *A Hermit of Carmel*. It included Santayana's own poetry and also his translations of poems by Michelangelo, the great artist of the Italian Renaissance, and Theophile Gautier, the 19th-century French poet. Scribners offered the book to the London publisher of *The Sense of Beauty*, but that publisher declined the offer on the basis that the poor quality of Santayana's poetry would discourage the public from buying his prose.

The following year, *Interpretations of Poetry and Religion* appeared, and it roused the fury of various factions. In this book, Santayana applied the theories he propounded in *The Sense of Beauty* to literary criticism. He declared that religion and poetry are essentially the same thing, a statement that upset the religious press. He also incurred the wrath of the literary world by attacking the poetry of Walt Whitman, Robert Browning, Shakespeare, and others. William James reported, however, that he had "literally squealed with delight" at Santayana's ability as a writer even while he disagreed with many of his positions.

After his controversial book was published, Santayana spent the summer at Oxford. Besides writing, he spent his time with an American horse dealer named Harold Fletcher, whom he had met six years previously. They went on drives through the English countryside for relaxation.

Several years later, Santayana found himself with a winter free from Harvard and began what must have been his grandest tour. This period was extended by lectures he gave the following year at the Sorbonne in France. During this two-year period, he traveled to Paris, England, Belgium, Holland, Germany, Florence, Rome, Naples, Sicily, Egypt, Jerusalem, and Athens, among other places.

Santayana muses in Hamburg, Germany, in 1907. In the early 20th century, Santayana traveled extensively, visiting Germany, England, Belgium, Holland, Italy, Greece, France, the Middle East, and Spain, before unhappily resuming his teaching duties at Harvard. During this time, he published his first major philosophical work, The Life of Reason.

He visited Susana in Ávila and spent three weeks in Jerusalem. With a trace of sadness, he noted that Turkish soldiers guarded the place where Jesus is said to have been born so that Christian groups would not fight over the shrine. He once wrote that he had dreamed of travel all his life; now he moved in fulfillment of those dreams.

Santayana eventually decided to abandon poetry in favor of philosophy. He had wanted more than anything else to be a poet. Certainly, he tried hard to succeed. He attempted to write many different kinds of poetry—satire, elegy, political commentary in verse form, lyric poetry, poetic drama, the sonnet, and other forms. Santayana was a hard critic of his own poetry and finally saw it as a failed endeavor. He would occasionally write more poetry, but never as much as before.

But Santayana was extremely pleased with the critical reaction to his next publication. In 1905 and 1906, *The Life of Reason; Or, The Phases of Human Progress* appeared in five volumes. The five volumes were *Reason in Common Sense, Reason in Society, Reason in Religion, Reason in Art,* and *Reason in Science.* The critical reception of the work was so great that *The Life of Reason* became a kind of bible in America for several generations of naturalist philosophers. The purpose of the work was to interpret the role of reason in the various activities of the human spirit. The combination of Santayana's scholarship and his gifts as a writer won the admiration of many. His intent was to evaluate the contributions made by common sense, social organization, religion, art, and science to securing the ideal life, one of happiness and reason.

Santayana began with the premise of naturalism, that everything, even ideals, has a basis in nature. He next described the patterns into which human activity falls as well as how human values and institutions developed. Santayana believed that human nature was not fixed but was evolving and that religion, art, reason, common sense, science, and society were created as responses by human nature to changes in the environment. Reason works to create harmony among our various impulses in order to create a world in which the gratification of these impulses would be guaranteed.

The acclaim won by *The Life of Reason* gave Santayana a position of strength when he was considered for promotion to a full professorship. In 1907, William James retired, and the situation was brought to a head. Santayana wrote to Eliot and informed him that if he was not given the position, he would resign. The threat worked, and Santayana was finally a full professor.

Now recognition on a national scale began to come to Santayana. He was elected to the American Academy and Institute of

Arts and Letters two years after his promotion to full professor. Eliot resigned the presidency of Harvard that same year and was replaced by Abbott Lawrence Lowell. Also around this time, Santayana's mother, well on in years, began to suffer chronic ill health. As she continued to deteriorate over the next three years, Santayana dutifully visited her. Toward the end of her life, he came daily.

The year after his election to the academy, Santayana published a new book, *Three Philosophical Poets: Lucretius, Dante, and Goethe*, a work honored by being published as the first volume of the *Harvard Studies in Comparative Literature*. Santayana wrote this new book as an application of theories he had put forward in *The Life of Reason*. The book was highly successful and established Santayana as a leading literary critic.

Santayana was still unhappy at Harvard despite the success and recognition he now enjoyed. He longed to be free of all obligations and duties so that he could follow his own thoughts wherever they might lead him. Moreover, Santayana desired obscurity, and the lessons of his crisis at age 30 were not forgotten. He continued to put money aside so that he could one day quit teaching.

In the spring of 1911 he wrote a letter to President Lowell and submitted his resignation, to be effective in a year. Lowell, who saw Santayana as the brightest star of the philosophy department, made a counterproposal to him. If Santayana would stay, he could have all the free time he wanted. Santayana accepted.

That year, Santayana traveled to Madison, Wisconsin, by train to accept an honorary degree of doctor of letters, an honor bestowed upon him by the University of Wisconsin. He continued on to California to deliver an address at the Philosophical Union of the University of California, a remarkable speech that included a history of philosophy in America. He pursued the theme to examine the impact of history on this country's intellectual life. In the speech, Santayana argued that the intellectual tradition in America was in a sorry state and that the intellectual heritage brought to

America from Europe had been altered and split off from daily life. He said that as a result America was able to produce neither genuine religion nor great poetry.

With his business in California completed, Santayana began his return journey to Europe. In New York he managed to see a play, have lunch, tea, and dinner, attend a ball, and see a musical before sailing for England. Shortly after arriving in England, he received a telegram that informed him of his mother's death. When news came that he would receive $10,000 from her estate, he decided to retire from Harvard for good and spend the rest of his life doing what he loved best—studying, writing, and traveling.

After he resigned his teaching post at Harvard, Santayana began work on his second major philosophical work, The Realms of Being, *and resumed a life of incessant traveling. During the 2-year period following his resignation, Santayana crossed the English Channel 21 times.*

CHAPTER FIVE

Disillusionment

Thirty-two months would elapse from the time he left America until the outbreak of World War I. During that period, he would cross the English Channel 21 times, shuttling back and forth between England and the European continent.

Santayana's love of travel did not prevent him from working, however. In a letter to one of his former colleagues at Harvard, George Palmer, two months after his resignation, Santayana described an idea he was entertaining for his second masterwork, *The Realms of Being.* He also reported that he had turned in a number of essays to his publisher. These appeared the following year, 1913, as a collection entitled *Winds of Doctrine.* A third work was also in progress, *Dialogues in Limbo.*

In this last work, the ghosts of the Greek philosopher Socrates and other men of ancient times are in limbo, the region between heaven and hell where, according to Catholic theology, the souls of the righteous who died before the coming of Christ are consigned. There they converse with each other as well as with the "Spirit of a

Stranger" still living on earth, Santayana himself. The book is a criticism of modern life and thought. Santayana felt that the classical virtues he believed in were ignored by the modern world. The give-and-take between the spirits is lively, and Santayana admitted that among his books *Dialogues in Limbo* was his favorite. It was finally published 13 years later.

Santayana toured Florence, Italy, and then moved on to Monte Carlo, where he visited its casino. He spent the Christmas of 1913 with Susana in Ávila. He went to Seville with his half sister and a friend of hers. They returned to Ávila a week later, but Santayana remained behind for Holy Week and to attend the bullfights.

In June 1914, an assassin triggered the events that precipitated World War I by shooting Archduke Franz Ferdinand of Austria-Hungary. With England about to declare war, Santayana had a sense of dark foreboding. Whatever the results of this war would be, he was sure they would be "hateful." Santayana tried to be as detached as possible about the war. This was in keeping with the philosophical stance assumed since his crisis at age 30, when he determined to renounce attachments. Still, he could not help but

Members of the King's Royal Rifle Corps parade down a London street in 1915 as part of a World War I recruitment drive. That year, Great Britain attacked Turkey in the Battle of Gallipoli, at the western end of the Dardanelles, the narrow strait that separates Asia Minor from Europe. The offensive proved disastrous for the British, who suffered some 200,000 killed or wounded.

British troops replenish munitions on a World War I battlefield in Belgium. San-tayana, who stayed in England during World War I, was ambivalent about the war: He believed in the Allied cause and loved England but sympathized with his home-land, Spain, which, although technically neutral, was decidedly pro-German.

feel somewhat ambivalent about the war. His heart was with the Allies, because he felt they favored individual freedom as well as "delightfulness of life." Nonetheless, his Spanish background intervened. Although Spain remained neutral throughout the war, it was pro-German in feeling, as was his half sister Susana. For a while, Santayana was unsure about where to spend the war. By the year 1916, he had become more anti-German in sentiment. He finally determined to remain in England throughout the war in order not to develop a distaste for his native land.

Although none of the terrible land battles of the First World War were fought on English soil, news of the violence had a great immediacy in that country. Santayana could not resist buying extra evening editions of the newspapers to follow the details of the horrific slaughters. It was a time of disillusionment for Santayana as well as for multitudes of other people, whether they were intellectuals or members of the working class. The era in which Santayana grew up, the 19th century, was one that believed strongly in progress. The intellectual revolution of the 18th century, the Enlightenment, had championed reason and science. Reverberations from the Enlightenment were still felt in the following century. Charles Darwin's theories about evolution were much discussed, and it was a common belief that the world would inevitably evolve into a more harmonious and peaceful place, given the blessings of reason. The degree to which Santayana was heir to this tradition is hinted at in the title of his five-volume work: *The Life of Reason.* The common faith in reason as the world's savior was made questionable, if not untenable, by the 30 million casualties of World War I.

Santayana found himself unable to work because of the war. That the England he so loved was suffering hurt him deeply. The country was also being changed in the process, and so he had to accept the loss of the England he had known and cherished in his youth. He abandoned writing philosophy but apparently could not stop writing entirely and returned to writing poetry. This time he wrote sonnets.

Edith Wharton, the American novelist, wished to help children who were victims of the war. She edited an anthology, *The Book of the Homeless,* to raise money for children who were orphaned or homeless. Santayana contributed a poem, "The Undergraduate Killed in Battle: Oxford, 1915." Among other well-known contributors to the work were Jean Cocteau, Thomas Hardy, and W. B. Yeats.

Not satisfied with contributing poetry to the war effort, Santayana turned to sharpening his best sword, philosophy. Santayana believed that the war was not caused so much by economic rivalry or political ills but by something unhealthy in the German metaphysical tradition. He criticized the emphasis that German philosophers had placed on will and the lack of objectivity in their

In an effort to raise money for children who were victims of the war, the American writer Edith Wharton edited a volume of poetry, The Book of the Homeless, *to which Santayana contributed a poem. A master of her craft, Wharton was best known for her novels and stories, in which she satirized American social and moral values.*

thinking. He wrote down this analysis of German thought and published it as *Egotism in German Philosophy.* Another work of Santayana's that was published during the war was the fruit of earlier writing. Before leaving America, he had written a number of articles about his travels in that land. These were published as a book in 1914, *Appearances: Notes of Travel, East and West.*

Although Santayana was deeply concerned about the state of the world, he continued to share lighter moments with friends and to make new acquaintances. One person Santayana met during the war was the great American novelist Henry James, brother of his former colleague at Harvard, William. It was reported that Henry James had said he would walk through a snowstorm for miles in order to meet Santayana. Mutual friends arranged a lunch so that

During the war, Santa-yana met the American writer Henry James, one of the greatest novelists ever to write in the English language and the brother of Santa-yana's teacher William James. Of James's many masterpieces of fiction, perhaps the best known is the novella The Turn of the Screw, *which he published in 1898.*

the two men could meet. James gave Santayana a warm welcome. Santayana wrote afterward that Henry had made him feel more comfortable and more completely understood over one meal than his brother, William, had over the course of many years.

Yet sad disillusionment was the predominant note of Santa-yana's life in England during the war. Preoccupied, he would take cheese, bread, and a notebook and spend the entire day walking by himself. The fruit of these solitary walks was a series of essays giving voice to his sadness. After the war, the essays were published in book form as *Soliloquies in England*. One commentator on Santayana called it Santayana's most nearly perfect work and expressed the opinion that Santayana was mourning not only England but his prior optimistic belief in reason.

Always on the move, Santayana left London for Oxford, where he became good friends with Robert Bridges, Poet Laureate of England. Bridges thought highly enough of Santayana that he tried to induce him to remain in England: Would Santayana like to be a lifetime member of his college, Corpus Christi, at Oxford University? Santayana declined. He still declared that he had "nothing to teach" and only wanted to learn. He would continue to travel.

Santayana's half sister Susana poses with her husband, Celedonio Sastre, in Ávila. Santayana, who supported the Allies in World War I, went to Spain after the war was over and visited Susana, who had supported Germany, and he found that their political differences put a strain on their relationship.

CHAPTER SIX

On the Move

Free again to move, Santayana spent summers in Paris, where his friend Charles Strong had an apartment, and winters in Rome, where he stayed in a hotel.

Between 1872 and 1912, Santayana crossed the Atlantic Ocean 38 times. His love of travel was not mere self-indulgence, however. He wanted to learn, "and with being eternally a student went the idea of being free to move." For Santayana travel was a normal activity that taught how different societies had evolved various beliefs about life and styles of living. Travel was, moreover, a way for him to maintain his cherished independence.

Santayana wanted to return to Spain soon after the war ended. Once there, he found that his support of the Allies had adversely affected his relationship with his beloved Susana and her family. Because of this disaffection, he returned to Spain only a few more times after World War I. In fact, he did not set foot in Spain during the last 24 years of his life. It is surprising that aside from his own family and one Spanish family he especially liked, his inner circle of friends never included a Spaniard. But he continued to follow events in Spain, especially political developments, and he would maintain his Spanish citizenship for the rest of his life.

Santayana now formed a daily routine that permitted him to think, write, and enjoy life as he traveled. He preferred to write in the morning, and he did so without dressing, working in his pajamas. He ate breakfast in private and dressed at lunchtime. On a typical winter day in Rome he would cross the Piazza della Minerva to buy a copy of *Il Messagero*, an Italian newspaper, and eat lunch in a restaurant. Next he went to a café for coffee and then returned to his hotel room and took off "such garments . . . as necessarily remind a philosopher of the sad fact that he has a body."

Santayana loved to eat gourmet food and drink fine wine, particularly with good friends such as Charles Strong. He would sometimes take the glass of wine and pour it over his cake. This startled one of his friends, who later adopted the same practice, however, after trying it. He began to receive many visitors after World War I and was said to be an excellent host. Always protective of his mornings, which he invariably set aside for writing, Santayana usually booked an extra room in his hotel for his guest and would not be available until lunchtime. All in all he was content with this manner of living, in which he balanced socializing with time for reflection. He remarked to a visiting friend, "My own room . . . is sacred, and I live happy in it, like a monk in his cell."

Santayana maintained a wide correspondence, and so letter writing was also a routine part of his existence. He kept in close touch with British and American friends. As well as writing to them, he answered correspondence from strangers and even sent them money on occasion. In 1929, he requested that $100 be sent from his account to an old man who wrote to him saying that Santayana should send him some money since he, too, was a poet.

In 1920, Santayana published a short work, *Character and Opinion in the United States*. This collection of essays was his farewell to the United States and to teaching. In addition to writings on political and intellectual traditions in America, the book contains two essays on his former colleagues, Josiah Royce and William James. That same year, a volume of Santayana's earlier writings appeared as *Little Essays Drawn from the Works of George Santayana*. The material in this volume was chosen and edited for the general public and gained wider recognition for Santayana. Now editors began to request contributions from him, and his essays began to appear in *Scribner's*, an American monthly magazine, as well as *Athenaeum*, a distinguished London periodical.

In 1921, the critic Owen Barfield called Santayana the greatest critic alive. Another respected critic, Desmond McCarthy, agreed in 1932 and said that no one was Santayana's equal "in measuring the minds of poets, novelists, and philosophers." An example of Santayana's sensitivity and insight as a critic is his remark about a work of Dante's concerning ideal love, the *Vita Nuova*: "The learned will dispute forever on the exact basis and meaning of these confessions of Dante. The learned are perhaps not those best fitted to solve the problem. It is a matter for literary tact and sympathetic imagination. It must be left to the delicate intelligence of the reader, if he has it; and if he has not, Dante does not wish to open his heart to him." John McCormick noted in his *George Santayana* that Santayana's criticism had as its foundation a solid knowledge of scholarship. McCormick further cites Santayana's wide knowledge of languages, aesthetics, and his intellectual range as qualities that made him a superlative critic.

In 1921, Santayana's half brother, Robert, died, and Robert's son, George Sturgis, took over the job of managing the philosopher's investments. He proved an able financial manager, and Santayana's worth multiplied many times. This affluence did not change Santayana's way of life. He did not spend his investments and only spent part of the profit from them. Instead, he applied most of his interest to the principal so that it could increase further. He lived mainly on money earned from his articles and books. By 1923, the year Scribners published his *Selected Poems*, demand for his

For years, Santayana's half brother, Robert Sturgis, served as the philosopher's financial adviser. When Robert Sturgis died in 1921, his son, George Sturgis, took over Santayana's finances, and the philosopher's assets increased under the young Sturgis's adept management.

books was growing. By 1927, his $10,000 inheritance of 1912 had increased to around $140,000. He spent only half his annual income of $7,000.

In 1922, Santayana abandoned Paris for Nice as his base for travel. The following year, he published one of his most pivotal philosophical works, *Scepticism and Animal Faith*. This work occupies an important place in the entire body of Santayana's writings because it was both a critique of his prior thought and the fulfillment of his previous writings. It was also a preparation for his seminal work, *The Realms of Being*.

Santayana set out in *Scepticism and Animal Faith* to disprove all theories of knowledge. The evidence of the senses cannot be trusted, he asserts, nor can logic or dogmatism give human beings an accurate understanding of the world. However, because people act confidently in a world that is dangerous, they must know more than such a skeptical point of view would allow. That is, individuals act as if they had absolutely reliable information about themselves and the world. Santayana calls this confidence that allows people to act "animal faith"; one writer has called it Santayana's form of common sense. We interpret the world around us by such animal faith, and life can thereby become meaningful. How we interpret the world is determined both by biological and social factors. Our interpretations (or beliefs) may not be ultimately correct, but thanks to them, people can live and enjoy life.

In *Scepticism and Animal Faith*, Santayana formulated a concept that is crucial to his entire philosophical system, his theory of essence. Santayana made a distinction between existence and essence. Essences include ideas, perceptions, possibilities, and meanings. The realm of existence includes things, people, and events. An example of an essence would be the concept of *pi* in geometry: Although one cannot know absolutely what pi is, one can still make use of it.

Santayana moved into a hotel in Rome in 1924 and stayed there until World War II. He always preferred to live in cities. While he might be "in exile," like the philosophers of classical times, similarly he would also be "in sight of the marketplace and the theatre." He loved Rome and considered it the one human dwelling place "where nature and art were most beautiful, and mankind least

La Chiesa della Trinità (Church of the Trinity) in Rome. In 1924, after many years of traveling the world, Santayana finally settled in Rome, which he called the city "where nature and art were most beautiful, and mankind least distorted."

distorted." During these years in Rome, he often went to Cortina d'Ampezzo, a village in the Italian Alps, to escape the summer heat.

The same year that he settled in Rome, his *Dialogues in Limbo* appeared serialized in a magazine. In 1926, it was published in book form. Around this time his nephew and financial manager, George Sturgis, came to visit him. He brought with him his wife, Rosamond. Santayana developed a deep affection for Rosamond, and they carried on a regular correspondence from 1926 until his death.

Santayana published two books the year after he met Rosamond: *Platonism and the Spiritual Life,* a long essay that set forth his ideas about spiritual life, and *The Realm of Essence.* The latter is the first volume of the four-volume work entitled *The Realms of Being.* The other 3 volumes were written and published during the next 13 years. The entire work is complex, and the individual books defy brief description.

The first volume is especially important for several reasons. The theory of essence was necessary to complete Santayana's system of philosophy. He had discussed his theory in *Scepticism and Animal Faith*; in the first volume of *The Realms of Being* he elaborated on it. This volume is so fundamental to the work that follows it that one commentator has said that the three succeeding volumes are simply notes to the first. The four volumes investigate Santayana's four major modes of being—essence, matter, truth, and spirit.

Central to *The Realm of Essence* is the distinction between essence and existence. The purpose of essences (ideas or perceptions) is to describe existence and help human beings understand it. In the category of existence, Santayana includes events, people, and things. *The Realm of Essence* expands his conception of essence as given in *Scepticism and Animal Faith* by describing how essences function in poetry, religion, history, and logical discourse.

In 1927, Santayana read an essay written on his work by Daniel Cory, a young American staying in England. Santayana invited his young admirer to visit and sent him money to cover the trip. Cory accepted the invitation, and thus began an important relationship that endured for the rest of Santayana's life.

With the large amount of writing Santayana produced, he always had a problem keeping his papers in order. He asked the younger man to assist him as secretary, and Cory accepted. Cory came to fulfill the role of editorial assistant to Santayana and, finally, became a confidant.

Although Cory assisted Santayana, he eventually became a burden to him. Santayana never intended to be Cory's sole financial support, but ultimately this became the case. Part of the time, however, Santayana shared Cory with his old friend of college days, Charles Strong, a philosopher himself and now in need of secretarial assistance as well. Strong had relocated by now from Paris to Italy.

Three deaths in Santayana's family during three years' time now shattered his tranquil life. First his half sister Susana died in 1928, followed by her husband, Celedonio Sastre, and then his other half sister, Josefina. The death of Susana, the person to whom he had been most attached, must have been a tremendous loss for

Santayana, his half sister Josefina (right), and Mercedes Escalera, a family friend, in Seville, Spain, in 1914. Susana and Josefina died within three years of each other, and Santayana, deeply saddened, took responsibility for settling their estates.

Santayana. Five years after her death, he wrote to console a friend whose son had died, and in the letter he acknowledged the pain of losing a loved one: "It is like a physical wound; we may survive, but maimed and broken in that direction; dead there."

Now legal and financial problems connected with Susana's estate came to bedevil Santayana. Susana had left $20,000 locked in a drawer. As a further complication, $5,000 of the legacy was to go to her brother Robert, who had already died. In rural Ávila, $20,000 plus the rest of Susana's holdings represented quite an estate. Servants, relatives, and heirs became anxious to receive their share and complained when they could not get their hands on it at once. Spanish laws were complicated in such a situation, and there were many bureaucratic requirements that exasperated Santayana. He wrote to George Sturgis in irritation, "Would your Aunt's property go to the government, or to the dogs, or to the Circumlocution Office?" Finally, the will was settled, and Celedonio Sastre's death the following year simplified legal matters somewhat. Santayana's connections with Spain were coming to a close.

With Santayana's fame and reputation growing, Harvard twice attempted to lure him back. First they offered him the Norton Chair of Poetry, one of Harvard's most prestigious appointments. Predictably, Santayana declined. He replied that his work on his books and essays left him no time to spare. Furthermore, he had grown so accustomed to retirement that he would "tremble" at the prospect of regular lectures. Sometime later, Harvard dangled different bait. Would Santayana return to accept an honorary degree and read an essay? No, he still refused to interrupt his routine.

The second volume of *The Realms of Being*, entitled *The Realm of Matter*, was ready for shipment to the bookstores in 1930. In this volume, Santayana states that matter ultimately cannot be known, for people can apprehend it only *through* essences. Matter is constantly changing, in a state of flux. Matter is such fertile material that it gives rise to complex entities such as the human psyche. The psyche "is made of matter as a cathedral is made of stone."

As the 1930s began, Venice became a regular stopping place in Santayana's never-ending round of excursions. The early 1930s also brought an unwelcome change in Santayana's life: Like countless others, he fell victim to the Great Depression, the very severe international economic crisis of the 1930s precipitated by the 1929 stock market crash. All of a sudden his worth was half of what it had been. Santayana considered his options. Should he move to a place where life would be less expensive? Should he accept the offers to lecture he routinely turned down? Santayana was fortunate, for he never really suffered during this time. He had more than he needed to live on, and the money he inherited from his sisters offset to some extent what he had lost.

The next work by Santayana to be published was *The Genteel Tradition at Bay*. His speech before the Philosophical Union of the University of California in 1911 finally bore fruit in the form of a book some 20 years later. In this work, Santayana intended to distance himself from an American school of belief, the New Humanism, which on the surface seemed to take positions similar to his own. The New Humanism school became prominent in the 1920s and counted among its followers Santayana's former student T. S. Eliot. The New Humanists rejected supernatural religion, romanticism, and much of modernism. Santayana felt obliged to criticize their works, for he found that their humanism lacked both depth and discrimination.

The year 1932 was the tricentennial of the births of the philosophers Locke and Spinoza. Santayana, now 69 years old, was invited to give public lectures at celebrations of each of their tricentennials. The Dutch government invited Santayana to speak on Spinoza. The lecture was given at The Hague, the seat of government. It was the Royal Society of Literature that invited Santayana to speak in London on Locke.

The Hague, in the Netherlands. In 1932, Santayana accepted an invitation by the Dutch government to give a lecture at The Hague. His topic was the 17th-century Dutch philosopher Baruch Spinoza.

This last lecture did not go as smoothly as Santayana had planned. First, he found the audience cool; then he was put off by Sir Rennell Rodd's introduction. It was obvious that Rodd knew nothing about Santayana's work or career. Next, Santayana had difficulty reading his speech. He had purposefully written it out in large handwriting so that he could read it easily. To Santayana's dismay he found that all the lights were focused in his eyes and none on the words he had to read. He managed with some difficulty to finish the talk after requesting that some of the lights be turned off. To Santayana's relief, the audience applauded warmly at the end. It is not surprising that Santayana had difficulty reading his speech, because his eyesight, which had never been good, had begun to fail.

Now, for the first time since World War I, Santayana published little. Instead, from 1932 to 1935 he concentrated on finishing a long-postponed novel. He had begun writing it as a story in college. When he finally completed the novel, he wondered "if any other book ever took 45 years to write." His method of working on the novel in the 1930s was to complete a draft of a chapter and then give it to a typist. The typed chapter was given to Cory for comment and suggested revisions.

The Last Puritan bears the subtitle *A Memoir in the Form of a Novel.* Since many of the novel's characters were based on friends still living, Santayana had considered not allowing the work to appear during his lifetime. His publisher's lawyers reassured him that a few minor revisions would protect Santayana from libel suits. Scribners submitted a distribution proposal for the work to the Book-of-the-Month Club, and it was accepted. This meant a wider readership for the book and more money in royalties.

The work was reviewed by many critics and favorably by the great majority of them. The *Saturday Review of Literature* called it "a book worth attacking, worth defending, worth digesting." Henry Hazlitt stated that "since Henry James there has been no American novel so rich in thought and analysis." Less favorable reviews maintained that the book was not really a novel but "just a front for an argument."

The title page from Santayana's novel, The Last Puritan. *The French inscription from Alain, a pseudonym used by the French writer Émile-Auguste Chartier, reads, "It is said that experience speaks through the mouths of the old, but the best experience they can convey to us is what they have preserved from their youth."*

THE LAST PURITAN

A MEMOIR
In the Form of a Novel

BY
GEORGE SANTAYANA

On dit bien que l'expérience parle par la bouche des hommes d'âge: mais la meilleure expérience qu'ils puissent nous apporter est celle de leur jeunesse sauvée.
ALAIN.

NEW YORK
CHARLES SCRIBNER'S SONS
1936

The novel is a character study of Oliver Alden, the last Puritan. In essence a tragic figure, Alden is ruled by a sense of duty. Indeed, duty can be said to be his lifelong motto. He even proposes marriage twice because of his feelings of duty. Much of the interest of *The Last Puritan* derives from the sharp contrasts between Alden and other figures in the book. Jim Darnley, for example, a yacht captain with an illegitimate child, becomes Alden's best friend. Mario Van de Weyer, Alden's distant cousin, is romantic and passionate in temperament, loving Italian ways. That Van de Weyer is poor but happy confuses Alden, who is an unhappy millionaire. When World War I begins, it brings changes for all and disaster for some. During the war, Alden finally manages to free himself of all duties just prior to the book's ironic conclusion.

Readers and critics wondered how much of Santayana himself was present in his characters. The author wrote to one person that *The Last Puritan* gave "the emotions of my experience, and not my thoughts or experiences themselves." Santayana wrote to Cory that "there was a hidden tragic structure in it which . . . belongs to the essence of the subject, the epoch, and the dissolution of Protestantism."

The novel was a considerable success. It was quickly translated into Swedish and German and later into Japanese, Danish, French, Spanish, and Italian. The English published a Braille edition, which caused Santayana to quip to a friend, "Me and the Bible." Santayana earned a lot of money from the sale of the book, which was on the best-seller lists for several weeks and was honored as one of three books awarded the *Prix Femina Americain,* a prestigious literary prize. Because of the book's notoriety, Santayana's face appeared on the cover of *Time* magazine. Nine years before, in 1927, Santayana received the Gold Medal of the Royal Society of Literature in London, but now he was truly an international celebrity.

Santayana spent some of the money earned from the success of his novel by booking a suite in a Paris hotel and treating Cory to a trip to Paris as well. Santayana wanted Cory with him to help prepare his next major philosophical volume. Santayana thought of others at this time also and put more money in his will for some family members and Cory. When his cousin Manuela died of gangrene, he sent money to pay her medical expenses. Others benefited from his generosity, including Mercedes de la Escalera, an old family friend who had become impoverished because of the civil war raging in Spain at the time. He also sent a friend in America $1,000 when she was hospitalized.

Not only did Santayana become known as the author of a best-selling novel in 1936; several other works of his appeared that year as well, including *Obiter Scripta* (Things Written Along the Way), a collection of lectures, essays, and reviews. In addition, Scribners published a large anthology of Santayana's works called *The Philosophy of Santayana: Selections from the Works of George Santayana.* Scribners had decided to publish a complete edition of Santayana's works, and the first 6 volumes of this 15-volume edition were already displayed in the bookstores. It had been by any standard a truly remarkable year.

Santayana in Rome in 1936, the year Scribners published the novel The Last Puritan *in New York. The book's success surprised Santayana, who, after a long and relatively obscure scholarly career, was suddenly thrust into the spotlight as the author of an international best-seller.*

CHAPTER SEVEN

Politics and Another War

Whereas the late 1930s may have been a time of accomplishment and acclaim for George Santayana personally, it was a time when Europe was making a rapid descent into violence. Strife was everywhere as Communists fought Fascists and the Nazi war machine prepared to crush Europe, Russia, and North Africa. Santayana's native country was also undergoing a particularly bloody civil war. Santayana was preoccupied with world events in general and with Spain in particular. Spain was extremely polarized after a decade of recession, student protests, burning of churches, threats of secession by Catalonia, revolution, violent strikes, and terrorism. The inevitable result was the Spanish civil war. It was a terrible war that resulted in some 1 million Spaniards losing their lives or fleeing the country.

When the war threatened Santayana's relatives in Spain, they naturally turned to "Uncle George" for help, and he did not disappoint them. He sent money continually as disaster and hardship struck his in-laws. When the home of his brother-in-law's family was

Fascist soldiers occupy a church reduced to rubble during the Spanish civil war. The Fascists, under General Francisco Franco, took control of the Spanish republic, and Franco became Spain's dictator in 1939.

bombed, he sent them money. He sent yet more money when the death of one family member left five children orphans. And Santayana's generosity was not limited to victims of war. He told his niece Rosamond that he would like to contribute $100 yearly to her son Robert during the time he was in college and that he preferred to do it anonymously. Santayana's philanthropy was not unusual; he regularly gave away a good amount of his earned income, some years as much as one-third. What he gave, he gave cheerfully, always saying that he was not at all depriving himself. At the same time, he spent little on himself. He seemed pleased to tell one person that he lived on less than a third of his income, "as a philosopher should."

If Santayana was generous, not all who received his gifts responded in the same spirit. In the late 1930s, he received a letter from a mutual friend saying that his cousin Bertrand Russell was financially embarrassed. Unable to find a position teaching in Britain, Russell, who loved to eat such delicacies as caviar, was poverty-stricken. Santayana wrote to his nephew George and proposed that a portion of the profits from *The Last Puritan* be given to

Nazi troops gather for a rally in Germany during World War II. During the war, Santayana became increasingly interested in world politics, particularly developments in his home country, Spain, which after a decade of domestic strife had fallen into the hands of the Fascists.

Russell anonymously. Santayana feared that "Bertie" would feel humiliated if he were aware that Santayana was supporting him. Russell, ignorant of the identity of his benefactor, complained that Santayana was a cold man. Eight years later, when Russell wrote *A History of Western Philosophy*, he snubbed Santayana in the text.

Ezra Pound, the highly acclaimed American poet and critic, was living in Italy at this time and wanted to get to know Santayana. Pound told Cory that he would like to send one of his books to Santayana. Santayana was annoyed and asked Cory to stop Pound from doing so, saying he abhorred "all connection with important and distinguished people." Apparently, his distaste for Pound's poetic style had something to do with Santayana's strong feelings. Still, he said if Pound needed money he would be glad to help him if he could do so without Pound knowing the source.

Pound finally managed to get his foot in the door, and when he did Santayana managed to warm up somewhat. By now Santayana was beginning to lose some of his hearing, however, and reported after one visit that he could not hear or understand half of what

Pound said. Pound had a pet project in which he wanted Santayana to participate. His idea was that he, Santayana, and T. S. Eliot would write a book with the purpose of proposing reforms in American education. Pound tried to convince Santayana that the book would be an ideal forum to answer his critics. Santayana was not interested. He said that he had no ideas on the subject and that he was "cynically content to let people educate or neglect themselves as they may prefer."

In 1938, Scribners published Santayana's *Realm of Truth*, an investigation into the nature of truth and how the material universe, truth, and essence are related. With the publication of Santayana's thinking about what constitutes truth, three of the four volumes of his last magnum opus, or great work, were complete.

In 1939 it was evident that a new world war might begin at any time and Italy would no longer be safe. Santayana cast about for a place to live. He tried to enter Switzerland but was turned back at the border. Santayana had not known that because of his Spanish passport, he would require a visa. When he traveled back to Milan to get one, he was told that he could have only a two-week visa. Switzerland had recently changed its regulations because many

Santayana's association with the American poet Ezra Pound has been the subject of controversy because of the latter's support of the Fascists in Italy during World War II. One of the most influential poets and critics of his day, Pound was admired by those familiar with his work, but he was widely criticized for his totalitarian politics.

Patrons relax at le Dôme, a popular Paris café in the city's Montparnasse section, during the 1930s. When Santayana was searching for a place to settle in 1939, he considered France, having enjoyed many summers there in the past, but he decided to settle in Italy instead.

refugees were fleeing the Spanish civil war. The Swiss asked him many questions about his politics, but he refused to answer. He would spend the summer in a familiar spot, Cortina.

Cory joined him there, and they worked on completing *The Realm of Spirit*. Convinced that war was imminent, Santayana pushed hard to finish the last volume of *The Realms of Being*. He was determined to mail the manuscript before any special postal restrictions came into effect. By now he had decided to stay in Italy during the war that now seemed certain.

In September, Santayana moved from Cortina into the Hotel Danieli in Venice. There Santayana resumed his normal routine, working on his writing all morning long in his pajamas and then taking a mile-long walk in the afternoon.

On June 10, 1940, the inevitable happened—Italy entered World War II. Santayana had expected Venice to be a safe haven, but less than three days after Italy's declaration of war, a port outside the city was bombed. Santayana soon left to take refuge in Cortina. After two months, the province surrounding Cortina was declared a military area off limits to foreigners. Santayana returned first to Venice and a month later to Rome.

When Italy declared war on the side of the Axis powers (Japan and Germany), Italians were asked to donate their medals to the war effort. In response, Santayana gave the medal he had received from the Royal Society of Literature.

The question of Santayana's support of Italian fascism has been much discussed. First of all, there is no doubt that Santayana was sympathetic to Italian dictator Benito Mussolini. Santayana was not a believer in democracy, and he took the Fascist position that the democracies would not have the will to fight the Axis powers. Although Santayana was never politically active for any cause in his entire life, some people felt that he was an active Fascist.

This impression resulted in part from his association with Ezra Pound. Pound had become obsessed with ideas about economic theories years before he met Santayana, and this fixation had led him to embrace the Fascist position. Pound was such a fervent supporter of Mussolini's that he made radio broadcasts from Rome supporting Mussolini's regime. In four of these broadcasts, he mentioned Santayana as if they were in general agreement on the issues of the day. Santayana in fact had already begun to wonder about Pound's sanity, telling him at one point, "I can't reply to your

The Nazi dictator Adolf Hitler greets adoring German masses during the late 1930s. Hitler rose to power while Germany was in the depths of an economic depression; in his rousing speeches he spoke of a Germany on the verge of greatness, and the nation was mesmerized.

suggestions and diagrams because I don't understand them." After the war, Pound was tried for treason and committed to an institution for the insane.

Santayana's defenders point out that many prominent people in the 1930s admired Mussolini. Like Franco in Spain, Mussolini arose in Italy after a turbulent period of strikes, riots, and general disorder. When Mussolini restored order, the Italian people welcomed his authority. Before he undertook the military conquests of other countries, Mussolini was hailed by many in Europe and America as a kind of superman and a genius.

Those who would exonerate Santayana point out that his distaste for democracy was like that of some classical Greek philosophers. Santayana wrote in an essay, "Classic Liberty," that for the Greeks liberty meant not only the freedom to live but, moreover, to live well. All the same, his long work on politics, *Dominations and Powers*, which he was writing around this time, never offers a practical alternative to modern democracy. No charge of support for Adolf Hitler's brand of fascism can be leveled at Santayana, however. In fact, the book he had written to oppose Germany in World War I was reprinted during the Second World War. Santayana even wrote a new chapter for this edition in which he attacked the Nazis.

Italy's Fascist dictator, Benito Mussolini, delivers an address at the Coliseum in Rome during the 1930s. Santayana's critics argued that the philosopher was sympathetic toward fascism and toward Mussolini in particular. Although he was not a champion of democracy, Santayana repeatedly criticized the Fascists in his writing.

Santayana's detractors urge that his political judgment in *Dominations and Powers* was thrown off by his "cynically low" appraisal of human reason and ability. They see in his political opinions a lack of care for human beings. One writer traces this to the materialistic bias in his political philosophy. As Santayana believed that forces in political life were material, he felt that only other material forces could influence them.

When Santayana, in 1950, addressed the question of his sympathy for Mussolini, he wrote:

> I was never a Fascist in the sense of belonging to that Italian party . . . a nationalist or religious *institution* will probably have its good sides, and be better perhaps than the alternative that presents itself at some moment in some place. . . . But Mussolini personally was a bad man and Italy a half-baked political unit; and the *militant* foreign policy adopted by Fascism was ruinous in its artificiality and folly. . . . Dictatorships are surgical operations, but some diseases require them, only the surgeon must be an expert, not an adventurer.

Santayana finished *The Realm of Spirit* in time to get it outside Italy before wartime postal restrictions made it impossible. When it was published in 1940, *The Realms of Being* was complete. By "spirit" Santayana meant thought or consciousness. He wrote that one of the hallmarks of spirit is its spontaneity. By virtue of its spontaneity, spirit can engender new ideas and provide a new vision and perspective for human endeavor. By providing discipline for our impulses, spirit can lead us to a harmonious and satisfactory way of life. Still, spirit has its own motives. For its fulfillment, it strives to unite itself with the will of everything that struggles.

Explication of this process of the liberation of spirit takes up most of *The Realm of Spirit* and includes a critique and analysis of the world's great religions and philosophies. Santayana believed that most religions and philosophies either chose a mystic path (which he saw as a denial of consciousness) or proposed a merely intellectual version of the truth. Santayana sought a third way that would combine the strong points of both while avoiding the weaknesses in each. The model Santayana proposed was a sympathetic embracing of the goals of every natural being. Santayana named this attitude charity. This allows the spirit its own good, which is love freed of both anxiety and desire.

The first year Santayana was in Rome, he stayed in a hotel. Then, in 1941, at the age of 77, he moved to the Clinica della Piccola Compagna di Maria, usually referred to as the Home of the Blue Nuns because of the color of the habit worn by the nuns who ran it. His traveling days finally over, Santayana settled down to complete the first volume of his autobiography, *Persons and Places*, a work he had been writing for some time. He warned his nephew and his publisher that the work would probably not be publishable for a long time. It was mostly satire and gossip, he said, and many of the persons he wrote about were still alive or had children who were alive.

When the book was completed, Santayana did indeed have difficulty getting it published. The first obvious problem was getting the work out of Italy during wartime. Scribners suggested sending two copies, one by airmail and one by ordinary mail. The Italian postal service refused both packages. Scribners wrote to the American ambassador to Italy. Could he help? Perhaps he could get the manuscript out in a diplomatic pouch, which would not be subject to inspection. The State Department finally responded that it could do nothing because relations with Italy had been suspended. Scribners asked Cory if someone at the Vatican could help. The Vatican assented to have it carried by the Irish poet Padraic Colum to America's embassy in Madrid. From Madrid it was forwarded on to New York.

War brought problems more serious than the post, however. Financial difficulties had already begun and would plague Santayana until after the war's end. Even when Italy had been a neutral country, Santayana had had trouble transferring funds from his accounts in England and America to Rome. Several times he had written checks, only to have them returned unpaid.

Santayana's financial status soon became even more precarious. The Blue Nuns had a center in the United States near Chicago. Santayana had his nephew George Sturgis make arrangements to give enough of Santayana's funds to the Blue Nuns in Illinois to pay his Rome bills. Eventually, this came to the attention of the U.S. government, which put a stop to it. Even though well off, Santayana had to accept the nuns' charity for the duration of the war, until he could pay them back.

Then the Book-of-the-Month Club expressed an interest in *Persons and Places*. However, there was a catch: They wanted to publish and distribute the first and second volumes together. The problem was how to get the second volume out of Italy. Other complications arose even before this one could be resolved. First the U.S. government became interested because of all the commotion over the work. The War Department called Scribners and inquired if any of Santayana's books had been translated into Spanish, German, or Italian. Santayana's editor tried to reassure the official on the other end of the line that all of his client's works were of a nonpolitical nature.

The next set of problems concerned greedy claims to Santayana's money. Santayana had consigned all of the royalties from his autobiography (as well as from all future books) to Cory, for money could not be sent to or from Italy. Cory was in America and struggling to get by without the funds Santayana usually gave him. Santayana had already stipulated that Cory was to be the first recipient of a fellowship he had endowed at Harvard. When George Sturgis learned that his uncle's autobiography had been selected by the Book-of-the-Month Club, he became very interested. He wrote to Santayana's editor saying that surely George Santayana did not intend for all of those royalties to go to Cory. This began a legal battle that would last for years, even beyond George Sturgis's death.

Work on the autobiography continued in spite of all these vexations. Santayana evidently enjoyed reminiscing. "Never have I enjoyed youth so thoroughly as I have in my old age," he wrote in *Persons and Places* about the writing of this work. The war had the effect in America of making Santayana a distant and mysterious figure. *Current Biography* began its entry on him in their 1944 annual, "Somewhere in Rome there lives a philosopher in his eighties . . ."

Santayana's daily routine was very austere. Although he wrote to many people, he saw few visitors and made no effort to meet other writers or philosophers. At times, days passed without his speaking to another person, and his favorite exercise remained taking walks. Although Santayana did not complain about rationing, he had no meat and no fuel during his last winter in Rome. He lost so much weight that his clothes did not seem to be his own. Perhaps his age allowed him to be more detached from this war than from the previous one he had sat out in England. He wrote to a friend that hearing of the war's horrors made him suffer, "but at my age, knowing that I am useless, I console myself with my books and my philosophy."

Fortunately for Santayana, there was a library in the clinic. As he perused its books, he naturally found many volumes on religion. He reread the entire Bible and some major theological works such as the *Summa Theologica* of Thomas Aquinas, the 13th-century Italian theologian and philosopher. The result was that he began to write a book on Jesus of Nazareth.

Back in America, Santayana's editor was still having trouble with volume one of the autobiography as concerns over libel continued. When they sent the book to press in 1944, Scribners had as yet no knowledge about the disposition of the second volume. Scribners would not have to wait much longer; on June 1, 1944, the Allies occupied Rome, and young soldiers began to seek out the famous philosopher.

An aging man of letters, Santayana takes a break from an afternoon walk in Rome in 1944. On this occasion, Santayana was fortunate to find a park with a bench that had not been appropriated by people desperate for firewood during the lean years of World War II.

CHAPTER EIGHT

The End of Isolation

Allied soldiers appeared at the doorstep of the Home of the Blue Nuns and asked for George Santayana. They had heard that the famed writer was living in Rome and wanted to meet him. One infantryman brought him a copy of *Persons and Places*, which Santayana not only had not seen but did not know had been published. Besides gifts of magazines, some presented Santayana with soap, cheese, tea, and other practical items scarce during wartime. Some asked for his autograph.

One of the military men who came to see him was his nephew George Sturgis's son, Robert Sturgis. Robert approached his great-uncle somewhat hesitantly because of his immense reputation. He was soon at ease, however, and found him to be quite approachable and witty as well.

Inevitably, the military men were followed by war correspondents, and articles about the aged philosopher as well as photographs soon began to appear in the world's newspapers. Santayana, ever the kind host, welcomed the soldiers. With his usual good humor, he reported that he was visited by scores of people he did not know "as if I were one of the ruins of Rome." Mail now began to get through, and soon Rosamond Sturgis was sending Santayana expensive delicacies from S. S. Pierce, a gourmet store in Boston, and Cory shipped him a package containing pajamas and bedroom slippers. His publisher did not forget him, either, and sent more food. Now he could enjoy his customary afternoon teas again with fruitcakes, cookies, dates, and figs.

Not all mail was as welcome, however. George Sturgis had died and F. H. Appleton had succeeded him as trustee of Santayana's money. Appleton hired a lawyer to continue the battle over the windfall royalties from *Persons and Places*. The lawyer wrote Santayana an angry letter stating that Santayana had put himself in a precarious position by transferring $9,000 worth of royalties to Cory. Santayana was furious. He could not believe that he was threatened by someone who was supposedly working for him.

If Santayana now had some small luxuries, he was still far from being able to live comfortably. More than six months after the Allies entered Italy's capital, food and coal for heat were still difficult to obtain. Electricity was so inadequate that most of the time the lights shone only dimly. To stay warm, Santayana spent his mornings in bed or bundled up in winter clothes. Still, despite having to wear

The black market in Rome during World War II. With the Italian economy in shambles and fuel and foodstuffs in short supply, countless cold and hungry people sought to obtain provisions for themselves and their families illegally and at exorbitant prices, and the black market thrived.

gloves, he did not stop writing. He could not even sit in his favorite public place to enjoy the sun, for the benches had been chopped up and carried off by people desperate for firewood. Santayana loved order and hated living in such conditions.

The afflictions of old age began to grow noticeably worse for Santayana. He now suffered from bad teeth, and his deafness was an even more acute problem. In spite of it all, he remained in good spirits. An army visitor reported how often he laughed and noted that Santayana expected him to join in the laughter.

Doubts now plagued Santayana about the second volume of his autobiography. He hesitated for a while, suffering pangs of conscience as to whether he had revealed too many secrets in its pages that would hurt and embarrass others. Finally, he decided to proceed with publication and sent the manuscript back to the United States with a master sergeant. The officer took it upon himself to write to Scribners and complain of Santayana's lack of funds. Santayana's editor acted promptly and had funds sent to Santayana by mail. The editor got in touch with other former Harvard graduates now in positions of authority. Arrangements were finally made for Santayana to receive $500 each month until the wartime restrictions were fully lifted.

As Santayana wrote the third and final volume of his memoirs, he began to feel better in spite of all these difficulties. He was also at work on other projects. His editor had learned from reading an interview that Santayana possessed unpublished poems and wrote to Santayana to inquire if he could publish them. Santayana replied that he did not want them published until after his death. Moreover, he was still working on translations of other poets' works that he wished to add to the collection of his own poems. As he continued to work, the second volume of his autobiography appeared in bookstores; it sold well, but sales were not as brisk as for the first volume.

During the war, the nuns at the clinic had tried to convert Santayana back to Catholicism, but even the mother superior finally acknowledged their failure. Perhaps the sisters had felt that he was ready to convert when they saw the old man reading the Bible and perhaps preparing for death. The fruit of his reading came to bear several years after World War II, when Santayana published *The Idea of Christ in the Gospels*. The book was an immediate success, selling out on the day of publication, and was promptly translated into four languages.

The work has been described as sensitive and insightful in its approach to the figure of Jesus. The book tries to refute the attempts of Protestant theologians to portray the Gospels as being historically true. Santayana took the position that the real power of Christ in history was as a poetic force. The only way to grasp the symbolic meaning of Christ is therefore through creative imagination. Santayana did not believe, however, that Jesus was an imaginary person; rather, some historical personality must have inspired the New Testament.

In 1943, as U.S. bombers leveled German cities, killing thousands of civilians, the American poet Robert Lowell wrote a letter to U.S. president Franklin D. Roosevelt announcing his refusal to serve in the armed forces. After spending time in prison for draft evasion, Lowell sent Santayana a copy of his book Lord Weary's Castle *in 1947, beginning a correspondence that would last until the latter's death. The book won the Pulitzer Prize that year.*

In September 1947, Cory moved to Rome for a while to be with Santayana and to help him with his work. That same year, the American poet Robert Lowell sent Santayana a copy of his book *Lord Weary's Castle*, which was soon to win the Pulitzer Prize for poetry. The two writers began a correspondence that lasted until Santayana's death. In the letters they exchanged, Santayana gave the young poet the benefit of his reactions to Lowell's poetry, and Lowell introduced Santayana to poets and poetic idioms that were new to him. As Lionel Johnson had done before him, Lowell wrote a poem in his honor, "For George Santayana." Santayana's daily life returned to normal when, in 1947, he could finally have complete access to his financial assets. To celebrate, he bought himself a tea set, a new desk, and a bookcase.

He continued to read widely and tackled Albert Camus and Jean-Paul Sartre, the French existentialists. He kept to his usual routine of reading, writing, and entertaining visitors. This happy state of affairs faded in 1948. Europe and Italy in particular were unsettled politically and economically in the aftermath of the war.

The French writer Albert Camus, whose work Santayana studied, was an important figure in the French existentialist movement of the 1930s and 1940s. The existentialists focused on the alienation of the individual in the modern world, the implications of the inevitability of death, and the problem of defining one's self in a world of few, if any, values.

One of the intellectual giants of the 20th century and the leading figure in the existentialist movement, the French philosopher, novelist, and playwright Jean-Paul Sartre developed the central existentialist themes in his philosophical treatise Being and Nothingness. *Santayana read Sartre's work, which immediately after its publication was required reading for every student and teacher of contemporary philosophy.*

This continuing condition distressed Santayana to such an extent that he began to experience difficulty writing.

He badly needed the bookcase because he had so little room for his books. Before Charles Strong's death he had kept most of his books at Strong's villa. Now the nuns allowed him to use the room next to his own at the clinic both to store his books in and as a kind of receiving room to greet visitors. Finally, he had so little room for storage at the clinic that he tore the pages out of books he did not intend to keep as he read them.

Santayana continued to receive packages of food and welcomed a limited number of visitors. As he received more and more of the beverages and snacks he loved, he shared them with the nuns who cared for him. Prominent visitors who called on Santayana in 1948 included the poet and translator of the classics Robert Fitzgerald, writer Gore Vidal, playwright Tennessee Williams, and the composer Samuel Barber. As always, Santayana's door was just as open, if not more so, to those who were not well known. One such visitor was an American student and admirer named Richard Lyon, whom Santayana befriended, paying his expenses during two weeks in Rome and acting as his personal tour guide. Lyon had written him an admiring letter from Texas. They had an important correspondence in which Santayana took the time to explain carefully the basic tenets of his philosophy and to assist Lyon in planning his studies.

Lyon relates that when he met Santayana, he soon learned that the old man was very visual. When, for example, Santayana asked him what he had done on the train to Rome, Lyon replied that he had read a book. Santayana said, "My heavens, at your age I would have been looking out the window, trying to catch impressions." Delighting as ever in architecture, he took Lyon to see some of his favorite architectural monuments in Rome. Those he showed the young American included the statue *Moses* by Michelangelo and the enormous pillars in the Sistine Chapel designed by Bernini, the dominant figure of the Italian Baroque period. Pointing out Bernini's ornate work, Santayana remarked that the young had difficulty appreciating the baroque.

Another visitor to Santayana was philosopher Corliss Lamont. He published this account of his meeting with the elder philosopher:

> [A nun] ushered me into a sitting room. Santayana in his dressing gown shuffled in and took me down to the end of the hall to show me the view of the old city wall. Then we went into his own simply furnished room for tea.
>
> We talked for two hours without interruption, as I asked him question after question about his philosophy. Santayana was in his late eighties at this time and not in the best of health, but he seemed to me exceptionally keen intellectually. Throughout our conversation I was impressed by how alert and sparkling were his eyes.

One person's attentions that were unwanted were those of Cyril Clemens, Mark Twain's nephew. Clemens liked cultivating prominent people, and Santayana had caught his eye in 1930. But Clemens's persistent attempts to associate himself with Santayana failed. In 1946, Santayana refused to allow Clemens to write his biography. In 1948, Clemens launched a campaign to have Santayana nominated for the Nobel Prize. Santayana wanted Clemens to stop it immediately. In a letter to Clemens, the humble Santayana listed four reasons why he opposed the project, and the last one was especially interesting: "In what science or art could I be said to have accomplished anything? Literature? Philosophy? It is doubtful." In *Scepticism and Animal Faith* Santayana had written, "My system is not mine, nor new." Santayana felt that his ideas had been discovered before by other great philosophers and theologians and that he was merely restating these truths.

In his mid-eighties, Santayana was mindful of approaching death. He wrote letters to set the record straight on his philosophical positions that he believed had been misunderstood. He sent money to Rosamond Sturgis instead of leaving it to her in his will. In that document, he left Cory his manuscripts, personal effects, personal library, copyrights, and royalties and named him his literary executor. (At Santayana's death, his estate was worth more than half a million dollars.)

Now the afflictions of old age worsened. In 1949, Santayana lost the sight in one eye and had great difficulty reading, even with the aid of a magnifying glass. In spite of all the physical problems, his old age appears to have been his happiest time. Writing his memoirs, living with few possessions, and enjoying the simple pleasures of life, he seemed to have found the contentment with life he had espoused in his philosophy. He had concluded at the time of his crisis at age 30 that by renouncing the possession of things in a material sense, he could possess them in spirit and truly enjoy them. "To possess things and persons in idea is the only pure good to be got out of them; to possess them physically or legally is a burden and a snare."

Dominations and Powers, Santayana's most comprehensive treatment of political questions, was published in 1951. As with so many of his books, this one earned widespread praise. The book's purpose was to distinguish which forms of government were good and which were harmful. After an examination of what governments have actually done in practice, Santayana proposed an ideal political system. His form of utopia would be a world government that would be authoritarian yet flexible, led by humane rulers.

In 1951, Santayana decided to remake *The Life of Reason* into a one-volume work. Santayana's weakening vision obliged him to work at a slower and slower tempo as time passed. He continued to read two newspapers a day, however, and followed with excitement the events of the Korean War. He also revised the third and last volume of his autobiography. Cory mailed the manuscript when it was finished, but only after agreeing to a condition imposed by Santayana that the book not be published before Santayana's death.

Santayana then began to read in earnest in preparation for a book he wanted to write on Alexander the Great. Santayana had long been interested in this significant historical figure who had conquered the world in the 4th century B.C. In his memoirs Santayana wrote that the Hellenistic period—that time between Alexander and Julius Caesar—was the period of history that most corresponded to his own feeling.

Over the years, Santayana had wondered about the question of his identity: To what extent was he Spanish or American? He wrote to one friend that he had a Spanish passport and was not legally an American citizen. Still, he paid taxes to the U.S. government, and "in practice" as a writer he was an American. To whatever extent he did have American associations, his Spanish passport was so important to him that he was careful never to let it expire. One afternoon in 1952, seeing that his Spanish passport needed renewing, Santayana went to the Spanish consulate. There he fell on its steps. Carried back to the clinic, he was diagnosed as having broken three ribs. Cory, who was playing golf in England when he received the news, rushed to Santayana's bedside. He was relieved to discover that Santayana's life was not in danger. In fact, while his body was healing, Santayana began translating a poem by Lorenzo de' Medici, one of the great Renaissance patrons of the arts. He even made a drawing in ink for a title page, should the translation ever be published.

For years, Santayana had suffered from stomach problems. Now he was diagnosed with stomach cancer, and by July 1952 the disease had already attacked his liver. In his final days, he could eat no solid food and suffered acutely.

Cory had to fight with the nuns to ensure that Santayana always had a sedative to relieve his pain. The nuns felt that it was better for Santayana to suffer because, according to their beliefs, this would lessen the time his soul would spend in purgatory. As a last resort, Cory told the nuns that if Santayana could not have morphine, he would remove Santayana from the clinic and change his doctor as well. The threat worked, and Santayana was given the drug.

On one occasion, a Catholic nurse who had been giving morphine to Santayana suddenly said that she would not do so anymore unless he called in a priest and confessed to him. Santayana would

George Santayana, who died of stomach cancer at the age of 88, devoted his life to learning and to human understanding. For him, as for all great philosophers, philosophy was not merely an academic pursuit but, as Jean-Paul Sartre said, "a profound attempt to embrace the human condition in its entirety." As one who not only espoused ideas but lived them, Santayana remains one of the most important philosophers of the 20th century.

have none of it and murmured, "I shall die as I have lived." (In fact, Santayana had warned Cory on several occasions not to believe any reports that might be made of a deathbed conversion.)

Finally, his suffering grew so great that the morphine was ineffective. The doctor prescribed a very strong dose of morphine and left. After it was administered, Santayana died.

Santayana's will did not indicate where he wished to be buried. The Spanish consulate in Rome assumed responsibility, as Santayana was still a citizen of Spain. The writer was buried without a religious ceremony in a tomb reserved for the Spanish in the Campo Verano Cemetery in Rome. A number of poets—both Spanish and American—wrote tributes to honor Santayana. The Spanish poet Jorge Guillen wrote "Huesped de Hotel" (Hotel Guest) in his honor. Wallace Stevens, Santayana's former pupil, wrote one of his best poems, "To an Old Philosopher in Rome," in his memory.

One year after Santayana's death, the third volume of his autobiography was published. At the end of the book, he offered his final diagnosis of the world's ills and a prescription for its cure. The modern world, he stated, has an abundance of science of a technical but superficial nature; it does not have self-knowledge. Society is mad with the idea of progress without really knowing where it is going or why. What is necessary in order to live sanely? In the first place, self-knowledge must be attained, as the Greek philosopher Socrates had taught. Furthermore, one must know enough about the world to be able to recognize what alternatives are possible and which of them favor one's true interests.

To the end of his own life, Santayana had remained faithful to the highest truths he had been able to believe in honestly, those of classical Greece. He had once said in response to a criticism of his work, "Ah, I know why my critics murmur and are dissatisfied. I do not endeavor to deceive myself, not to deceive them, not to aid them in deceiving themselves. They will never prevail on me to do that. I am a disciple of Socrates."

Chronology

Dec. 16, 1863	Born George Santayana in Madrid, Spain
1865	Family moves from Madrid to Ávila, Spain
1869	Santayana stays with his father in Spain while his mother and two sisters move to Boston
1872	Family reunites in Boston
1873	Father returns to Ávila
1874–82	Santayana attends Boston Latin School
1882–86	Attends Harvard; studies philosophy under William James; graduates summa cum laude
1889	Receives Ph.D. from Harvard; begins teaching philosophy there
1894	First book, *Sonnets and Other Verses*, is published
1896–97	On leave from Harvard, Santayana studies philosophy at King's College, Cambridge
1904–6	Extensive travels in Europe and the Middle East; Santayana lectures in France while on leave from Harvard; *The Life of Reason* is published in five volumes

1907	Santayana promoted to full professor at Harvard
1912	Mother dies; Santayana resigns his post at Harvard
1912–14	Extensive European travel
1914–18	World War I; Santayana spends war years in England; writes *Egotism in German Philosophy*
1920–41	Travels throughout France, Spain, Switzerland, and Italy
1924	Rome becomes base for travels until World War II
1927	Santayana meets Daniel Cory; awarded the Gold Medal of the Royal Society of Literature
1928	Death of half sister Susana
1935–39	Santayana becomes a best-selling author with *The Last Puritan*; Spanish civil war
1939–45	World War II
June 1940	Italy enters World War II
1941	Santayana moves into a nursing home run by the Blue Nuns in Rome
1944	*Persons and Places*, volume one of his autobiography
June 1944	Allies occupy Rome
1945	*The Middle Span*, volume two of his autobiography
1946	*The Idea of Christ in the Gospels*
Sept. 26, 1952	Santayana dies in Rome of stomach cancer

Further Reading

Arnett, W. E. *Santayana and the Sense of Beauty*. Magnolia, MA: Peter Smith, 1984.

Cardiff, Ira, ed. *Wisdom of George Santayana*. New York: Philosophical Library, 1964.

Cory, Daniel. *Santayana: The Later Years*. New York: George Braziller, 1963.

McCormick, John. *George Santayana: A Biography*. New York: Paragon House, 1988.

Santayana, George. *The Complete Poems of George Santayana*. Edited by William G. Holzberger. Lewisburg: Bucknell University Press, 1979.

———. *Dialogues in Limbo*. New York: Scribners, 1926.

———. *The Idea of Christ in the Gospels or God in Man*. New York: Scribners, 1946.

———. *The Last Puritan: A Memoir in the Form of a Novel*. New York: Scribners, 1936.

———. *The Life of Reason; Or, The Phases of Human Progress. I. Introduction and Reason in Common Sense.* New York: Scribners, 1905.

———. *The Life of Reason; Or, The Phases of Human Progress. II. Reason in Society.* New York: Scribners, 1905.

———. *The Life of Reason; Or, The Phases of Human Progress. III. Reason in Religion.* New York: Scribners, 1905.

———. *The Life of Reason; Or, The Phases of Human Progress. IV. Reason in Art.* New York: Scribners, 1905.

———. *The Life of Reason; Or, The Phases of Human Progress. V. Reason in Science.* New York: Scribners, 1906.

———. *Persons and Places.* Edited by William G. Holzberger and Herman J. Saatkamp, Jr., with an introduction by Richard C. Lyon. Cambridge: MIT Press, 1986.

———. *The Realm of Essence; Book First of Realms of Being.* New York: Scribners, 1927.

———. *The Realm of Matter; Book Second of Realms of Being.* New York: Scribners, 1930.

———. *The Realm of Truth; Book Third of Realms of Being.* New York: Scribners, 1938

———. *The Realm of Spirit; Book Fourth of Realms of Being.* New York: Scribners, 1940.

———. *Scepticism and Animal Faith.* New York: Dover Publications, 1955.

———. *Soliloquies in England and Later Soliloquies.* New York: Scribners, 1922.

———. *Three Philosophical Poets.* Garden City, NY: Doubleday, 1953.

———. *Winds of Doctrine.* New York: Scribners, 1913.

Sprigge, Timothy. *Santayana: An Examination of His Philosophy.* New York: Routledge, Chapman & Hall, 1974.

Stallknecht, Newton P. *George Santayana.* Minneapolis: University of Minnesota Press, 1971.

Woodward, Anthony. *Living in the Eternal: A Study of George Santayana.* Nashville: Vanderbilt University Press, 1988.

Index

DAVID CARTER grew up in Jesup, Georgia, studied at the Sorbonne, in France, and graduated from Emory University in 1974. He holds an M.A. in South Asian studies from the University of Wisconsin–Madison. A specialist on South Asian religions, he wrote and directed a film documentary on the Indian spiritual master Meher Baba.

RODOLFO CARDONA is professor of Spanish and comparative literature at Boston University. A renowned scholar, he has written many works of criticism, including *Ramón, a Study of Gómez de la Serna and His Works* and *Visión del esperpento: Teoría y práctica del esperpento en Valle-Inclán*. Born in San José, Costa Rica, he earned his B.A. and M.A. from Louisiana State University and received a Ph.D. from the University of Washington. He has taught at Case Western Reserve University, the University of Pittsburgh, the University of Texas at Austin, the University of New Mexico, and Harvard University.

JAMES COCKCROFT is currently a visiting professor of Latin American and Caribbean studies at the State University of New York at Albany. A three-time Fulbright scholar, he earned a Ph.D. from Stanford University and has taught at the University of Massachusetts, the University of Vermont, and the University of Connecticut. He is the author or coauthor of numerous books on Latin American subjects, including *Neighbors in Turmoil: Latin America, The Hispanic Experience in the United States: Contemporary Issues and Perspectives,* and *Outlaws in the Promised Land: Mexican Immigrant Workers and America's Future.*

PICTURE CREDITS